# The Right Formula

Manchester University Press

# The Right Formula

## The Story of the National Graphene Institute

By David Taylor

Manchester University Press

Published by Manchester University Press
Altrincham Street, Manchester M1 7JA

www.manchesteruniversitypress.co.uk


British Library Cataloguing-in-Publication Data
A catalogue record for this book is available from the British Library.


Library of Congress Cataloging-in-Publication Data applied for.


ISBN 9781526113931        paperback

First published 2016

Designed by Aurélien Thomas, Jestico + Whiles
Printed by Gutenberg Press Limited, Malta

# Foreword

Graphene is an extraordinary material.

It is stronger than diamond, more flexible than rubber, and the most conductive material ever discovered. The initial scientific excitement has quickly been picked up by engineers, industry and the wider public as it became clear that graphene could transform technology and change our lives.

The original 'Eureka moment' of isolating graphene was astonishingly simple and yet elegant – peeling perfect crystals of graphene from a piece of graphite with sticky tape – and it has fascinated people all around the world. But big ideas and discoveries require extraordinary levels of support. That's why the Government was quick to act with funding for what is now the National Graphene Institute at The University of Manchester.

It took almost three years of hard work for architects, builders, scientists, local authorities and the Government to create what has become a truly remarkable achievement; not only in architectural terms, but in a new approach to science and technology.

The National Graphene Institute is 7,825 square metres of collaborative space dedicated to scientists and industry working side by side on the applications of tomorrow. Already over 50 commercial organisations from around the world are partners of the National Graphene Institute, working to bring graphene devices to the market. These partners include some of the world's biggest companies alongside small and mid-sized British firms, whose creativity, vision and expertise will help make sure things discovered in Britain get made in Britain.

In October 2015, I had the pleasure of accompanying President Xi Jinping of China on a tour to the NGI as part of his state visit to the UK, and was proud to show him a shining example of how the UK is capitalising on its world-class science with world-class investment. But what creates new ideas, new technologies and new partnerships is not buildings but people. Sir Andre Geim and Sir Kostya Novoselov, who were awarded the Nobel Prize for Physics in 2010 for groundbreaking experiments regarding graphene, lead more than 235 researchers in graphene and 2D materials. It is so heartening to see that, only a few months after I had the pleasure of opening the Institute, it is full of young talent from all over the world, bursting with ideas in a wide range of scientific endeavour. It is a vindication of why we provided funding for the National Graphene Institute and other graphene projects.

Of course this Institute is only the start of the Government's commitment to graphene. The £60m Graphene Engineering Innovation Centre is set to be completed in 2018 and will accelerate bringing applications to market. This will be followed by the £235m Sir Henry Royce Institute for Advanced Materials Research – a cornerstone of the Northern Powerhouse that will allow the UK to grow its world-leading research and innovation base in advanced-materials science, which is fundamental to all industrial sectors and the national economy.

Graphene is a brilliant example of what can happen when the Government backs science. It's why in the Spending Review we decided to protect today's £4.7 billion science resource budget so it rises with inflation for the rest of the Parliament.

I am convinced that the National Graphene Institute will be a perfect case study of how the UK can lead the world not just in science and research, but in commercialisation as well, and I look forward to many more exciting discoveries in the years to come.

George Osborne, Chancellor of the Exchequer

# Contents

Introduction     **11**

The Discoverers     **12**

The Discovery     **18**

What is Graphene?     **24**

The Aftermath     **28**

The Building     **34**

Making The Veil                    62

The Engels' Sink                   82

From Seathwaite                    86

How the Building Works             92

The Future                        110

Selected Publications             116

# Introduction

It all began with a piece of Sellotape.

In a corner of a laboratory building in Manchester in 2003, two scientists were messing about, indulging in a little blue-sky 'Friday evening' thinking. This was one of their regular sessions, designed to 'push envelopes' and stimulate a little left-field investigation. They had rescued some Sellotape that had been used to clean a piece of graphite stone from the bin, sticking it and unsticking it to and fro with another piece in a way reminiscent of taking fluff off a jumper. Until, finally, it all got serious. Here, eventually, was a piece of substance – of carbon – that was only one atom thick. This was a two-dimensional crystal. This was the world's thinnest, lightest and strongest material. This was graphene.

The scientists in question were researchers at The University of Manchester – Professor Andre Geim and Professor Kostya Novoselov. Later, in 2010, they would be awarded the Nobel Prize in Physics and knighthoods for their pioneering work – in formally identifying a material that was super-strong, extremely electrically conductive and might have many uses and applications far beyond their thoughts then, and even our dreams today. And it would lead too to the creation of the National Graphene Institute in Manchester, designed by architects Jestico + Whiles to help investigate this wonder material more and help the commercial sector to establish further quite what its scope can and should be.

But first, a bit of background.

# The Discoverers

'It is much easier to solve a problem
if you first guess possible answers.'

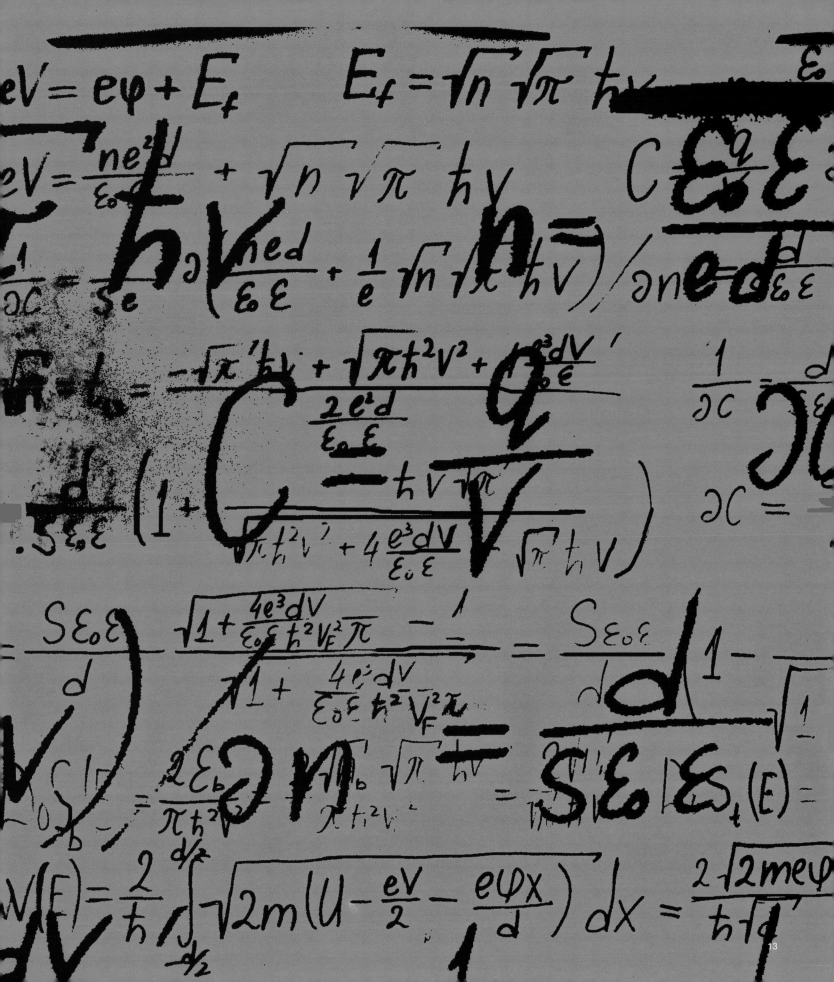

Professor Andre Geim was born in the small Black Sea resort of Sochi in 1958. He spent the first seven years of his life brought up by his grandparents, after which he joined his Volga-German parents and brother in Nalchik in the foothills of the Caucasus Mountains. It was only when he was 30, however, that Geim discovered that nearly everyone in his family had spent many years in the Gulag, and that some had been prisoners in German concentration camps. His 'ethnicity', would have a considerable bearing on his life to come.

Geim's early education benefited from his school's excellence in mathematics, physics and chemistry, and Geim once won a regional chemistry Olympiad thanks to memorising a 1000-page Chemistry dictionary. This was clearly no ordinary boy. After graduating at 16 with a gold medal for achieving a perfect score in all subjects, he opted for Physics at the Moscow Engineering and Physics Institute (MIFI). But he would come up against prejudice and was failed entry, largely due to his ethnicity, so found work in the factory his father worked in as a technician, responsible for calibrating measurement equipment. Meanwhile he paid for tutoring in maths, Russian literature, and physics, where his tutor provided a valuable life-long lesson. 'It is much easier to solve a problem if you first guess possible answers', wrote Geim in his self-penned autobiography to accompany his Nobel Prize win. 'This is the way I learned to think then and I am still using it in my research every day, trying to build all the logical steps between what I have and what I think may be the end result of a particular project.'

After another dispiriting knock-back at his next attempt to join MIFI, Geim despaired at the apparent discrimination against the ethnic minorities but applied successfully to Phystech – an institution 'two notches higher', where he would benefit from being taught by practising scientists from the region's Academy Institutes. Geim graduated with a 'red diploma', meaning he was in the top 5-10% of his class, but he recalls that he adopted an attitude of 'doing alright to reach a goal' rather than trying his utmost. When, however, he became an independent researcher, looking into the electronic properties of metals and developing his further experimental skills, Geim rediscovered his motivation and determination to do his utmost. This attitude and the skills he had learned would come greatly into play when it came to the graphene story.

Geim's reputation for playful curiosity-driven science is demonstrated by his original research prior to graphene. He remains the only person to have been awarded the Nobel and IgNobel prizes, given in 2000 for his levitation of a frog, and had previously come up with Gecko tape, a material so adhesive it mimics how the lizard clings to surfaces. 'In my experience, if people don't have a sense of humour, they are usually not very good scientists either,' he said. With mesoscopic superconductivity, diamagnetic levitation and four Nature papers to his name, Geim was beginning to be highly sought after in academic circles. By now at Radboud University Nijmegen, Geim's next move would be pivotal, and he was not short of offers. His principal reason for choosing Manchester was a simple one; his wife Irina Grigorieva, then a part-time teaching lab technician in Nijmegen and now an eminent physicist, was also offered a post at Manchester. It was an easy decision and, as Geim says in his autobiography, one they have never looked back on.

Professor Kostya Novoselov was born in Russia in August 1974, graduating from the Moscow Institute of Physics and Technology before doing a PhD in Holland and moving to Manchester in 2001. An amiable, thoughtful man with a glint in his eye and an occasionally mischievous air, Novoselov remembers fondly his youthful aptitude for science (albeit if even now he and his colleagues debate long and hard what is and isn't science) and making things. 'Yes, I was reasonably technical from the very beginning, he says, with characteristic understatement.

He grew up in the Urals in Nizhny Tagil, an industrial city where railway carriages and the T34 tanks – the mainstay of the Soviet army during WWII – were produced. In fact, he even worked in the factory that produced them during the summer holidays, aged 14. One of his more memorable jobs there was to help heat-treat large sections of the tanks in a huge bath. Clearly this was a kind of chemical and scientific investigation, even then, but there was more to this early brush with mechanics and mechanicals. Novoselov's father was into auto sport, particularly carting, and Kostya recalls riding motorbikes and driving cars from the age of around six. 'I even started to work on mills and lathes when I was quite little to make those parts.'

Certainly, not every child gets bought a German model railway as a gift but thinks that the best part of that present was its variable DC power supply. Novoselov did though, when he was just eight, and used it for all kinds of experiments for many years to come, including electrolysis and building electromagnets.

Novoselov's parents spotted this early ability, and pushed him to go for Science Olympiads, where he did well, reaching the all-Soviet level with his problem-solving ability, mainly in physics. The Distance Learning School of the Moscow Institute of Physics and Technology (Phystech) followed, but this was during a period of 'bad time' in Russia in the turbulent years between 1991-95, Novoselov remembering how he took part in one of two coups, the October Putsch. 'How we were not killed that night I still don't understand', he recalls. 'I came home in the morning and said, 'Gosh, I will never, ever participate in any revolution, ever again.' As a consequence of this experience, Novoselov decided that, from that day hence, his own revolutions would be in physics, rather than politics.

The tough times then meant little in the way of food, and lecturers at the university even brought in cookies for students to keep them going. Quickly though, things improved and Novoselov started work as a construction worker on flat roofing jobs. A managerial position followed hard on its heels, before he left to go back to serious study, even if academics at the time had little in the way of funding. At Chernogolovka, a small town in the middle of a forest around 60km east of Moscow, Novoselov revelled in the enthusiasm and passion for science shown by staff and students at the town's dozen research institutes. Here he would learn from some of the best minds, leading scientists at the Institute of Solid State Physics, the Landau Institute for Theoretical Physics and the Institute of Microelectronics Technology.

Professor Andre Geim offered an even bigger draw, however. In 1997, while Novoselov was working on his PhD in Dubrovski's laboratory, Geim, who had a reputation for being an 'innovative and creative experimentalist' and knew about Novoselov through mutual friends, invited Novoselov to study as a PhD student in Holland. He jumped at the chance. Novoselov spent a couple of months during the spring of 1999 in Nijmegen as what he calls a kind of 'probation period' before starting his PhD with Geim in the high magnetic field laboratory that August. This gave Novoselov the experience of working in a large, international laboratory with a huge variety of projects, but it proved to be a short-lived affair. When Geim moved to Manchester in 2001, it left Novoselov without a supervisor, so when offered a postdoctoral position by Geim – he didn't think twice and moved to England in 2001. His PhD would have to remain unfinished for the second time.

## The Discovery

---

'Graphene's key property is that it exists.
Full stop'

Those Friday evening experiments capitalised on testing dogmas in the fields outside one's mainstream activity. Without such curiosity-driven research, says Geim, there simply are no discoveries.

Unencumbered by the weight of expectation or dogma, they could freely ask questions from left field. The graphene discovery came while they were doing some work on superconductivity and ferromagnetism, so this was certainly a side experiment.

It happened like this. The standard test object for scanning tunnelling microscopes they were working on at the time, together with Oleg Shkliarevskii, was graphite, principally because it is easy to cleave thus efficiently cleaning the surface from contamination. But because you are imaging atoms, what you want, says Novoselov, is absolutely clean surfaces without contamination. 'So what people do usually is put on some Scotch tape and peel it away with the contaminated surface layer and then you get a freshly cleaved surface, which is very clean, and then they use that for their experiment'.

Then it was simply a matter of picking up this Scotch tape with pieces of graphite on it from the bin, and trying to extract some thin graphitic particles. 'It did work and we saw some transistor effect, and we thought it might be worthwhile to go further – to try to get thinner and thinner pieces'. The first samples were 20, maybe 30 layers thick, and all the experience from general physics and nanotechnology at the time told them that it would be impossible to get to one atom thick fabric because it would be unstable. 'But then, after a while we got it thinner, and thinner, and thinner', Novoselov recounts. 'And then we managed to do it!'

Lattice model depicting graphene's structure

A certain amount of luck is involved with many scientific discoveries. Here it was through the fact that the substrate used – the thickness of silicon oxide on top of silicon – was such that the one atom thick graphene could be seen through a microscope. But graphene's key property, says Novoselov, is that it exists. Full stop. 'The fact that it exists really sparked other 2D materials' he says. 'Now graphene is taken for granted and this shift in the perception really happened some time ago. And it was quite a shift for many people.'

There are lots of superlatives condensed into one material, however, such as its status as the strongest material, the most conductive, optically transparent but at the same time optically active... This is quite peculiar. But it is also an absolute game-changer.

Thin graphitic flakes on a sticky tape

Graphene flakes

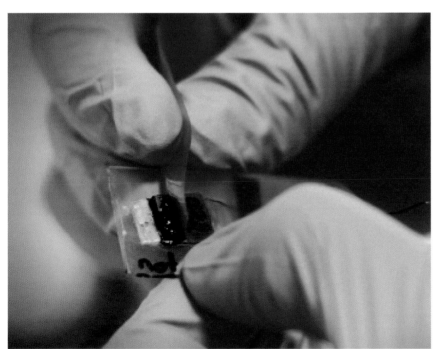

# What is Graphene?

By Kostya Novoselov

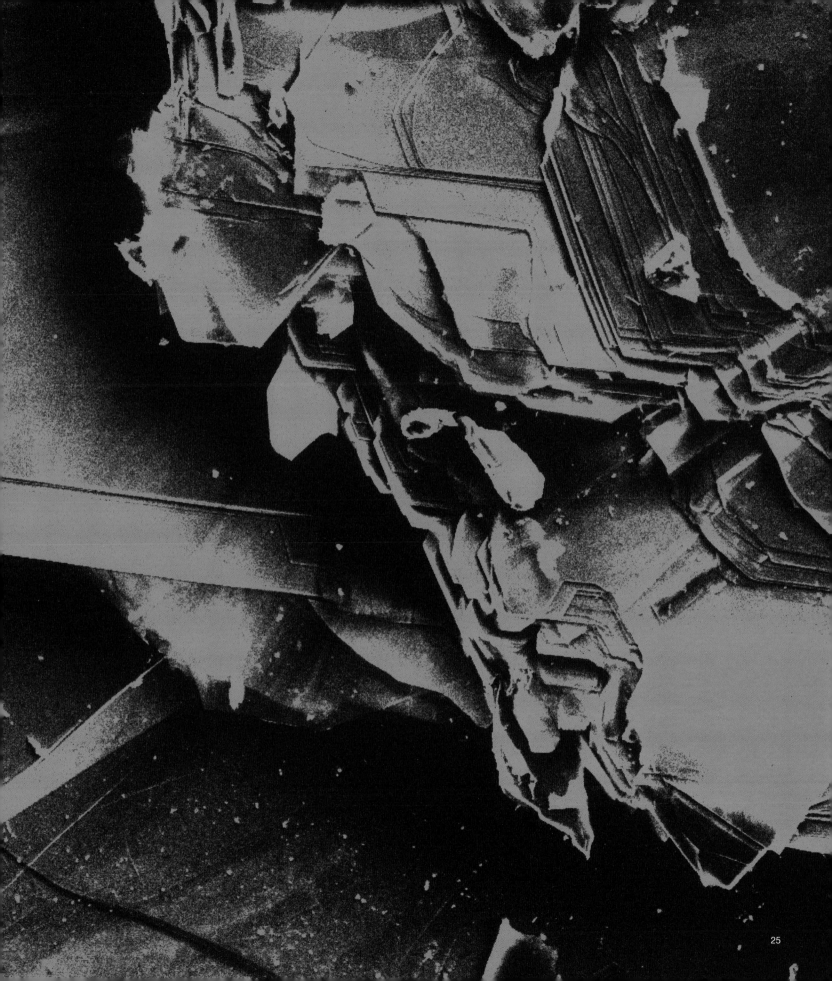

# Graphene

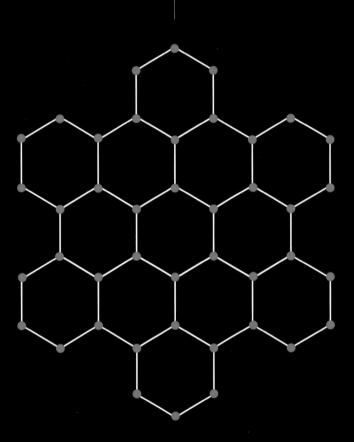

Graphene is 100 times stronger than steel

Graphene conducts heat better than any other material

Graphene, being one atom thick, is very transparent. And yet, it is optically active, absorbing 2.3% of light that lands on it

Graphene is a form of carbon consisting of planar sheets which are one atom thick

Graphene can support the highest current density, a million times that of copper

Graphene stretches up to 20% of its length but is also the stiffest material – even more so than diamond

Probably the most exciting property of graphene is its very existence. Graphene is exactly a one-atom thick layer of carbon. General wisdom tells us that such objects are very unstable, and yet graphene exists, it is extremely strong, very conductive and impermeable to any gases – to name just a few of its superlatives.

Electrons in this two-dimensional crystal behave very differently compared to other metals. They mimic massless relativistic particles – the property which earned graphene a nickname 'CERN on a desk'. Such unusual electronic properties led to the discovery of a number of exciting quantum phenomena.

Graphene possesses probably the largest number of superlatives, compared to other materials. It is the thinnest material possible, and at the same time, one of the most impermeable. It is very thermally and electrically conductive, extremely strong and elastic. It absorbs 2.3% of incident light (though this is quite a lot for a one atom fabric). All such properties prompted its use in a number of applications.

Graphene's transparency and high conductivity will find its use in devices requiring transparent conductive coating. Such devices include touch panels, solar cells, liquid crystal displays and many others. The unusual mechanical properties of graphene mean that such devices can be made to be flexible as well. Graphene's strength is being utilised in tough composite materials; its conductivity in ultra-fast electronic applications and batteries; its impermeability in water purification and the possibility of functionalising large surface area in medical applications, to name just a few.

Still, one of the most important properties of graphene is that it has opened the way for many other two-dimensional materials to be discovered and studied. The family of such one-atom thick crystals is now very large, numbering several dozen members. More importantly, such materials cover a very large spectrum of properties: from the most insulating to the most conductive; from optically active to very transparent. Also, very often the properties of such one-atom thick crystals are very different from their three-dimensional counterparts. Studying those properties leads us to the very exciting physics of two-dimensionality. Having such a variety of materials with a large spectrum of electronic, optical and mechanical properties further increases the range of possible applications. Still, even more interesting opportunities arise when one starts to combine these materials. It is possible to stack these one atom thick crystals into a three-dimensional heterostructure whose properties would be a combination of the individual components. This opens new horizons in the area of material engineering – creating materials on demand with atomic precision.

# The Aftermath

'Science fiction was becoming
science fact, and the world was
sitting up and taking notice'

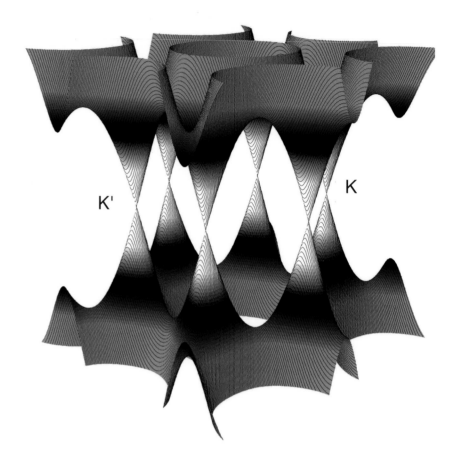

The electronic spectrum of graphene is characterised by linear dispersion relation around special points in the Brillouine zone

These 2D crystals can be assembled in 3D heterostructures that do not exist in nature and present unique physical properties

Andre Geim and Kostya Novoselov had begun working on graphene in 2003. The pair published their first paper in 2004, after which interest in the material spiralled exponentially. Science fiction was becoming science fact, and the world was sitting up and taking notice.

'It was a whole year of continuous excitement', Novoselov recalls. Popular culture of course likes to think of a 'Eureka' or light bulb moment, but really, behind that Sellotape incident it was a continuous affair, day and night in the lab, measuring, discussing, and measuring again. The difference was the intensity. 'For a typical piece of work novel results and experiments come maybe on a weekly or daily basis', says Novoselov. 'At that time it was on an hourly basis.'

Their typical work was in a broad spectrum – semiconductors, superconductors, ferromagnets included, plus a few more of those Friday evening experiments. Once the research on graphene had started, for several years it was all around this material. However, graphene research has many facets: they worked on its mechanics, optical, chemical, transport properties and many other topics. 'It was all very exciting', says Novoselov.

By the time Geim and Novoselov received the Nobel Prize in 2010 they were moving on apace with graphene. In particular, they figured out that graphene is not alone – there are many materials that are one atom thick. It is a huge challenge to select the ones to study, as all of them are very exciting, says Novoselov. Furthermore, these other materials, they discovered, could be combined together to gain properties they do not have when on their own. At the same time, the research on graphene applications intensified dramatically: Manchester now had a large community of researchers working in different aspects of graphene applications. So, after the discovery, it was time to create the right environment in which the next chapter in the history of graphene could begin to unfold.

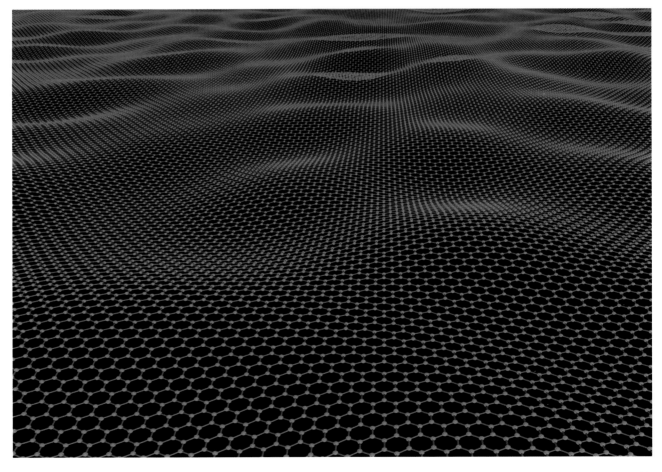

Researchers working in the optical lithography room

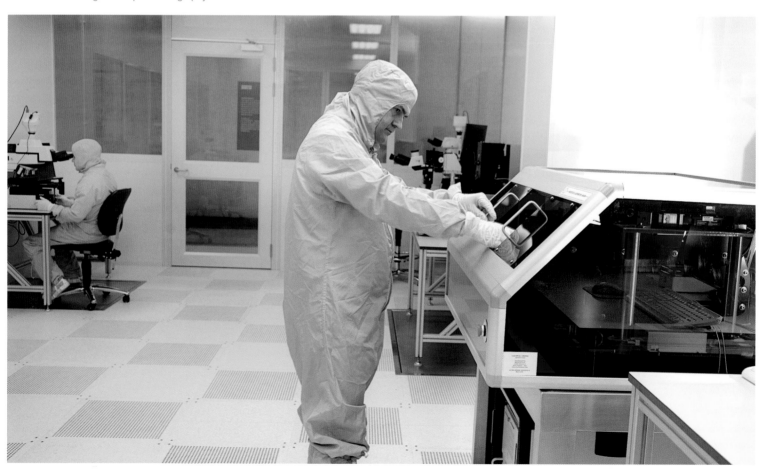

Production of graphene by centrifugation of chemically exfoliated graphite

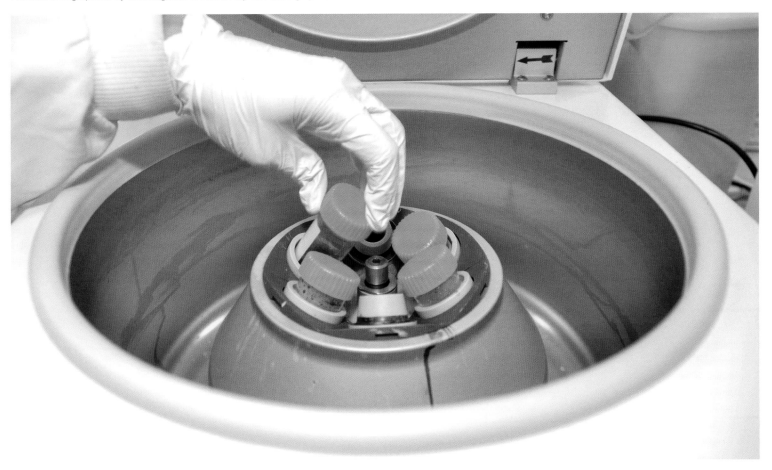

## The Building

---

'We always understood it
is a building of probably
unrivalled complexity'

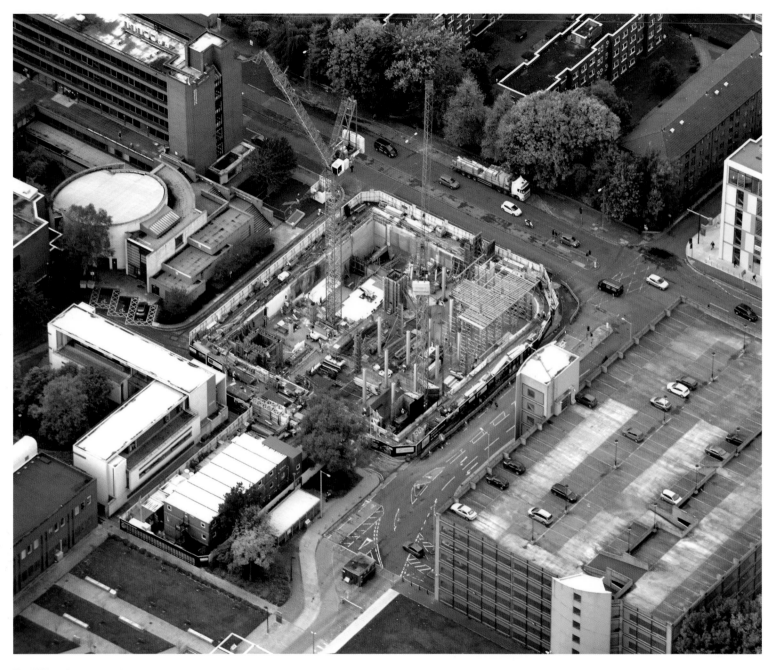

The NGI under construction

## The context

Manchester needed to capitalise on its ground-breaking discovery and create a fitting home for more work to be undertaken in graphene's name.

This was the city, after all, which gave this new wonder material to the world. It needed an iconic new presence for the science behind graphene, and an important landmark in the heart of the emerging 'Northern Powerhouse'. The small cleanroom in the university's old premises where Geim and

Thin film deposition equipment in the Centre for Mesoscience and Nanotechnology

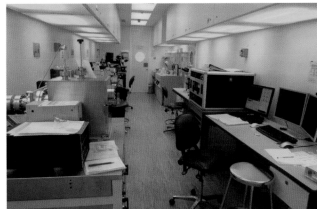

Optical lithography equipment in the Centre for Mesoscience and Nanotechnology

The site

Novoselov's teams were previously working served not only as a technology centre but also a melting pot for ideas. Staff and students from the university's departments of chemistry, physics, material science and others would all gather there to exchange their thoughts. But with around 30 professors working on graphene – which translates to around 200 students in total – there was a pressing need to replace the out-dated, overcrowded cleanrooms in the old facility. At the same time, it became obvious that there was more and more commercial interest in graphene. So having a new building was their chance to score twice - to start with a clean sheet and enable researchers to become more involved in collaborations with the private sector. Everybody wins.

The vision for the National Graphene Institute (NGI) came from the close relationship between key figures at the University, including President and Vice-Chancellor Professor Nancy Rothwell, the then Vice-President and Dean of the Faculty of Engineering and Physical Sciences, Professor Colin Bailey, and the city of Manchester, particularly its Chief Executive, Sir Howard Bernstein.

The university owned a small, developable plot of land in the centre of the University Campus' Science Quarter, and needed a building with cleanrooms and laboratories. It also needed space to house existing equipment, new items for new experiments into the wonder material, and staff from many different university departments. Happily, the university also secured the enormous fillip of a £61 million grant from the European Regional Development Fund (ERDF) and the UK's Engineering and Physical Sciences Research Council (EPSRC) as well as personal backing from ministers like George Osborne and David Willetts to contribute to a new building which might marry the twin goals of commercial and scientific achievement. In fact, graphene has already brought the city an estimated £175 million in investment so far. It was a highly-significant time for the University's Estates team, involved in managing a £1 billion ten-year plan to create a world-class University campus, constructing buildings for teaching and research and major improvements to the public realm. The NGI was the most complex project the team had managed. So, selecting a design team with the expertise and track record to build a scheme that dealt with all of the complex technical requirements would be the crucial next step to take.

The Mountbatten
Building, University
of Southampton

## Choosing the team

A little like a scientific experiment, the process of
assembling the project team was intensive and thorough,
and needed the right mix to make it a successful venture.
Following a feasibility study by a different design team,
the project was tendered through an efficient method for
clients, a framework then called The Government
Procurement Service (GPS).

Arcadis, formally EC Harris, was one of the framework
members and emerged victorious in the process for the NGI
ahead of the feasibility study team, largely based on the
experience and knowhow of its team members. The winning
team included Jestico + Whiles as architects, CH2M as
technical architects, services and mechanical and electrical
engineer, Ramboll as civil and structural engineer, and EC
Harris as quantity surveyor and project manager.
Jestico + Whiles could usefully point to its track record in
teaming up with CH2M on successful research laboratory
projects, including the well-regarded Mountbatten
Nanotechnology Research Centre for the University of
Southampton and the AIN-Physics Building for the
University of Sydney. CH2M, too, has a pedigree in high-
tech clean room laboratory design, with 30,000 worldwide
staff working on projects in labs and health care, industrial,
and programme management. 'To be honest, we always
understood it is a building of probably unrivalled
complexity', says Novoselov.

There are not many buildings in the world at this level, since
industrial cleanrooms are built with specific equipment in
mind. But here the task was made more complex still
because the brief was to build a complicated building for
a largely unknown set of equipment, and, more pointedly,
an unknown scope of research. The building should be able
to support the science for the several decades to come and
what we all like about science – that it is impossible
to predict what will come out of it. Flexibility was thus
a key watchword.

On the client side there were important players in all of
this too, of course, driving the direction of design for the
building and guiding its facilities to cater for the requirements
of its users. From the academic wing of the university these
included Prof. Ernie Hill and Dr. Peter Blake and from the
University's Estates side important figures like Stuart
Lockwood, Diana Hampson and, later, John Whittaker.

When it came to its construction, the NGI was a two-stage
design and build contract, with the winning contractor BAM
North West appointed to work with the EC Harris-led design
team for the 7,800m² building on its construction phase
between July 2013 and March 2015. But first came its design.

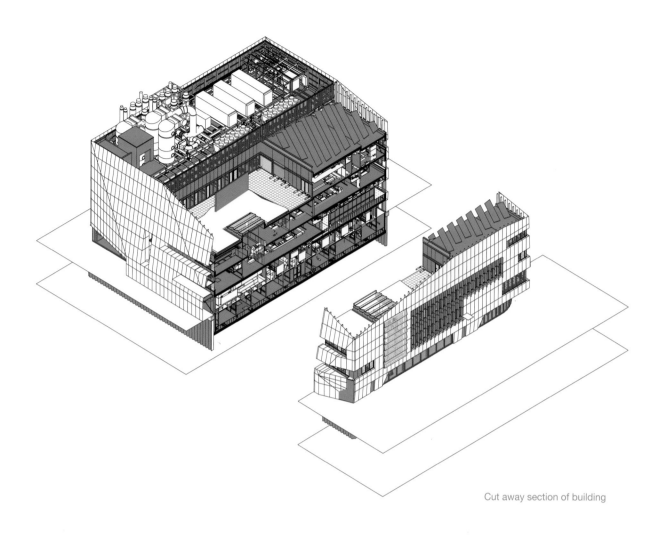

Cut away section of building

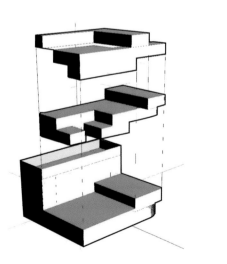

Interlocking volumes of cleanrooms, labs and offices

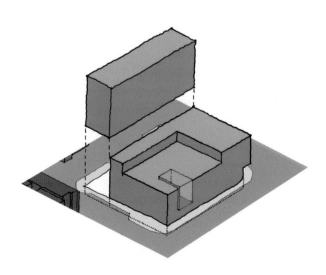

Separate structure for the CUB

A typical 'grey space'

Cleanroom

Return air and
service chase
in cleanroom

### Design fundamentals

Essentially, there were two key moves in designing the scheme; fundamental principles from which the rest of the design evolved.

The first involves vibration. For its cleanrooms to be a success, the NGI had to be a building which provided an extremely stable environment despite sitting on a busy road and needing unusually extensive servicing to heat, cool, ventilate and light it. For this reason, the decision was made to dig down and locate the main cleanroom on the bedrock, five metres below ground, where the effects of the road and all that heavy equipment could be minimised. 'That set the tone for how the rest of the building design would emerge', says Tony Ling of Jestico + Whiles. 'The rest falls into place, more or less.'

It was a solution proposed by the project engineers Ramboll, and involved substantial excavation. The desire for a balance between vertical stiffness for vibration control, layout and economy, meanwhile, resulted in the adoption of a 6.6m x 6.6m structural grid.

The second key move concerned the Central Utility Block or CUB, a section that is structurally isolated from the main building. Much of the building's plant is located here, again to minimise transfer of the kinds of vibration and noise levels that could disrupt experiments. The CUB is in effect the engine room of the building, a crucial component in making sure it runs as efficiently as possible.

A 50mm gap between the CUB and the main building allowed the creation of two independent structural frames within the scheme and ensures that vibration from the plant and lifts is not transferred to the scientific working environment. Situated to the west of the scheme and adjacent to the cleanrooms at basement and first floor level, the CUB is around a third of the width of the main building but rises to four storeys like the rest, and contains all of the mechanical, engineering and processing plant that is needed to make it work – items like air handling units, chillers, generators, substations, processing plant, and supplies of water, gases and storage.

Open plan laboratory
sketch (above)
and completed
image (below)

## Silver service

It was a tough brief, say the CH2M team, which supplied
the complex mechanical and electrical engineering thinking
in what is one of the most heavily serviced buildings
in Europe.

The technical requirements of the research environments
were, in the words of C2HM's technical architect
Bob Hedivan, 'complex and onerous'. The advanced
conditions, equipment and systems and working
arrangements of the research activities led the design
direction and determined much of the building form's
rationale. And, with a high degree of interface and
interaction required between the users and the designers,
this was perhaps the purest kind of form following function.
It was rather like a Ferrari in this respect, they suggest.

The building includes optical, electronic, chemical and other
laboratories. Professor Novoselov stipulated that these
needed to be environments that can be easily adaptable for
as yet unknown future experiments and equipment and
interspersed with offices to make it easier for researchers to
communicate and discuss their findings. Elsewhere,
ancillary accommodation includes a seminar room that
opens out onto a roof terrace with bio-diverse roof garden.
This features some 21 different grasses and wildflowers
designed to attract urban bees and other pollinators.
Hedivan feels that the scheme is an efficient project of its
kind which maximises its interior requirements, flexibility via
its servicing, grey space (more on this later) and oversized
lifts, and, importantly, its attractiveness as a place in which
to work.

By intermingling the offices and labs on all floors, individual
research teams at the institute have all the facilities they
need to operate coherently in one area. Those teams
include industry partners, who collaborate on research
into graphene and its myriad potential uses with
the university academics.

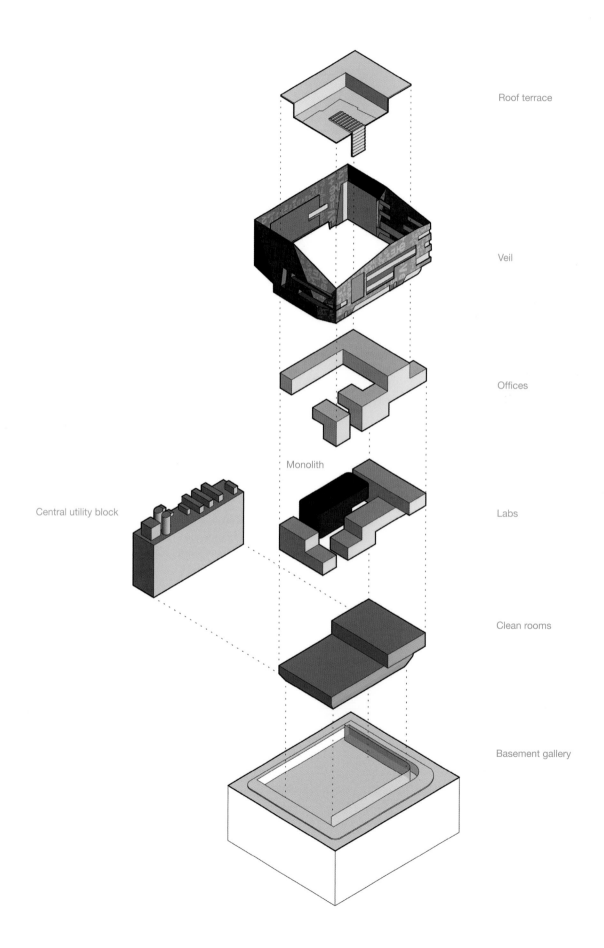

Roof terrace

Veil

Offices

Monolith

Central utility block

Labs

Clean rooms

Basement gallery

## Future proofing

On the client side, the personnel involved understood that they would have to influence the mindset of the architects, says Novoselov, to work with all the 'unknowns' imposed in future. Could the scheme be future-proofed as much as possible? That was the continuous challenge for both the researchers and the architects. Architects tend to work to a specific brief, but here that may change in three years' time. 'You also cannot underestimate the robustness of the university system – introducing changes into the building once it is constructed is a complex and lengthy process', says Novoselov.

But they persevered, ending up with a design which catered to as many of the desires as possible.

One of the key strategies employed towards flexibility to cope with all of this change was to instigate a system of laboratories and grey space. This allows a section of around 2.5m wide service space alongside the labs, across the whole building, which also provides storage and shelving as well as accommodation for some equipment – and it avoids cluttering up the labs. It also means that the scientists can use the grey space in which to keep some of the noisier equipment. 'Every lab has at least one wall which is backed up to a grey space', says Ling. 'We had successfully explored and implemented this concept at the Australian Institute of Nanoscience in Sydney.'

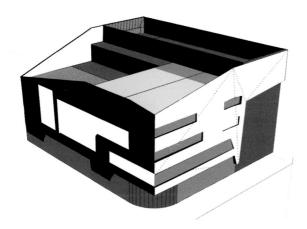

The concept of an external skin

Computer generated image of external skin concept, in situ'

The completed building

## Clear thought

Added to flexibility, though, another issue was transparency. Cleanrooms tend to be very unpleasant places in which to work. Those who do work there are dressed from head-to-toe in gowns, goggles, gloves and masks, and they have to spend many hours in the same labs. Usually, cleanrooms feel isolated and inward-looking. And in winter the staff might arrive at work in the dark and leave in the dark, without ever seeing the light of day. Dreary.

So the architects sought to bring daylight and views into the cleanrooms by positioning windows 3 metres below ground via a perimeter viewing corridor. In other words, unlike many 'black box' labs elsewhere, staff and students at the NGI can enjoy their context and retain a fix on time through witnessing the changing light conditions outside.
This daylight aspect is also true of most of the labs upstairs in the building. 'You can work for months without seeing the daylight', says Novoselov. At the same time, says Ling, people can see in, which helps to demystify the scientific process in action. 'That's important, and it is a big attraction, but it is crucially important for those who work inside', said Novoselov.

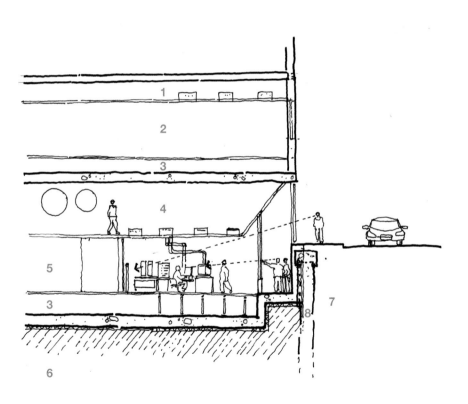

**Cleanrooms section**

| | |
|---|---|
| 1 Plenum | 5 Lower cleanroom |
| 2 Upper cleanroom | 6 Bedrock |
| 3 Raised access floor | 7 Piling and retaining wall |
| 4 Walk-on plenum | 8 Insulation and waterproofing |

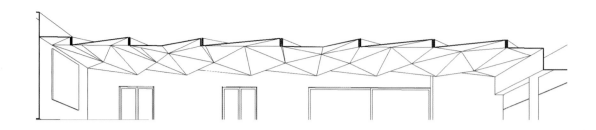

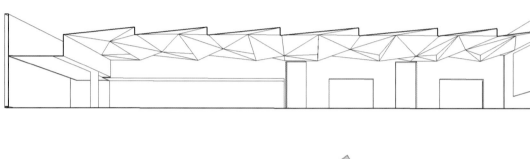

Writable wall at design concept stage (above)
and as constructed (below)

## Off the wall

How important are the social spaces within the building? It is often suggested in similar higher education buildings that these are where the real discoveries are made, through the interaction of staff and students alike, bouncing ideas off each other. Even to the extent that Novoselov was keen on having just one coffee machine in one place to encourage people to gather; in the end, two were installed. At NGI, the circulation spaces are also designed with this in mind.

The NGI's 'writable walls' are one of the most important features in this social aspect of the building and form a place for scientists to scribble down their ideas when inspiration hits. They consist of walls on two floors in corridors around the central block of labs, and are clad in a black PVC material. This was initially going to be a blackboard, but chalk was declared a banned substance for health and safety reasons. The obvious alternative was whiteboard, but the problem there was that they seldom remain in pristine condition after even a few uses. Another issue was the pens – it is difficult to erase erroneous workings on formulas and the like until the ink is dry. No such problem with the specific chalk-type pen now used on the PVC – the substance dries instantly, and the walls have become the centre for discussion and intellectual exchange.

The way the public 'read' the building's exterior walls was next on the design agenda.

Double height central
breakout space

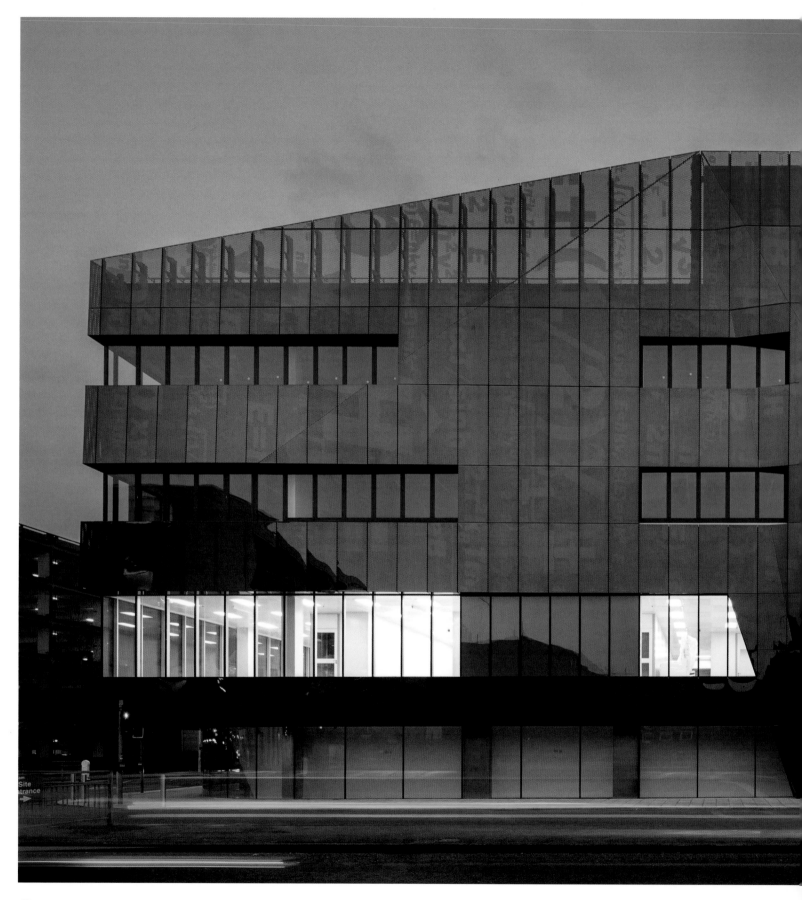

## Making The Veil

'It's got almost everything, and
when the sun goes down you see
the whole building change colour.'

The building's façade – its outward message to the city – was the subject of much deliberation and debate. Jestico + Whiles' Tony Ling recalls how his team of architects went through many iterations of its design before they were happy, considering many materials along the way. It had to be just right. 'We were looking for something that would be unusual and appropriate for this building', he says. 'We looked at all kinds of materials – copper, Corten, anodised aluminium, stainless steel, but nothing quite captured the mysterious quality that we wanted'.

In the end, the architects devised a double skin system, with the outer element made of Rimex, a 2mm-thick, mirror-finished black stainless steel dipped in acid, which offers a chameleon-like quality to the building. It changes the surface colour's appearance from a mirror-like jet-black to, even mid-way up the building, a much lighter colour as its reflections change. Or as it picks up the greens and greys of the nearby James Chadwick School of Chemical Engineering Building, for example. 'It's got almost everything, and when the sun goes down you see the whole building change colour', says Ling. A post-rationalisation of this would suggest this feature of the façade could be a metaphor for graphene itself, in terms of its flexibility and adaptability to different settings and scenarios.

But integrated into the façade, the architects would come up with a far more direct connection still.

## Formula won

Professor Novoselov himself spent long hours around the table doodling and mulling over the message this veil cladding could or should be making. Myriad options that were discussed and debated included graphene or non-graphene-related ideas, and scientific, literal or totally abstract patterns. Then there was the professor's hand-written version of his own equations for a graphene tunneling transistor, which were trialled but deemed not 100% satisfactory.

Finally, it was suggested that a more formal, typewritten version of the equations could be used, rotated at 90 degrees, and complete with overlapping sections. A subtle, graphical representation of the chemical make-up and equations of graphene is writ-large on the building's perforated veil. Even this went through much iteration, with long discussions amongst the project team about how subtle or otherwise these graphics should appear, and in what form.

Novoselov used formulae from their early graphene papers and even playfully added several jokes. But perhaps the biggest message of this veil to the building is true to the whole of science as it is to graphene – that nothing is as it first seems, and effort and hard work is required if solutions are to be found or discoveries made.

Finally then, a format for the veil was agreed. To create it, the Rimex sheet was laser-cut into different-sized holes but using the same centre point to make up the graphene equations when viewed from afar. 'It's a simple but clever principle', says Ling. 'There's a completely normal orthogonal grid, and it's only by varying the size of the holes that the equations can be read. There was a lot of work before we discovered that!' The 'veil' also acts to hide the extensive services at the rear of the building. That was something of a late headache for the designers, says Ling, with space needed for a chemical store, pumps, and the not inconsiderable requirement for several liquid nitrogen tanks, of which the largest is 7m tall with a 6000 litre capacity. 'So all of a sudden we had all these lumps which were added on to the back of the building.' Either these would be left exposed or a new wrap or skin for the building could enclose them. The veil was the answer, and the building design was complete.

As fellow graphene researcher James Tour of Rice University Texas commented in a New Yorker article on the subject: 'What Andre Geim and Kostya Novoselov did was to show the world the amazingness of graphene.' The architects wanted to convey at least some of this 'amazingness' through the imagery and materiality of the NGI.

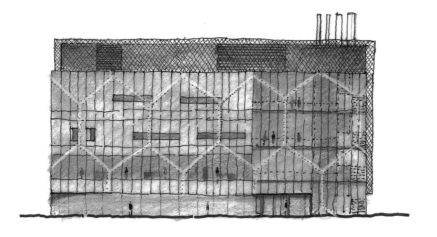

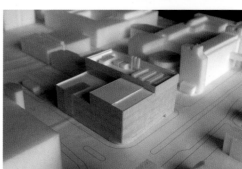

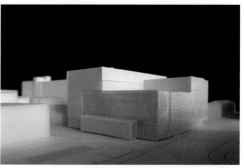

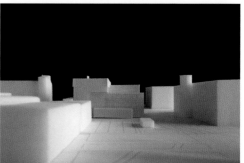

Early design studies of façade

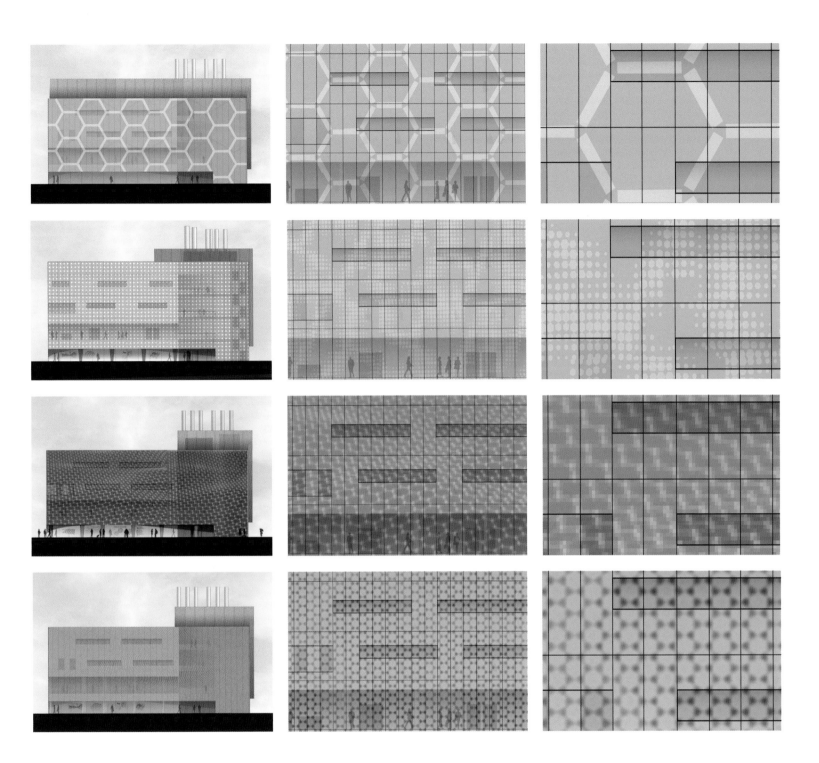

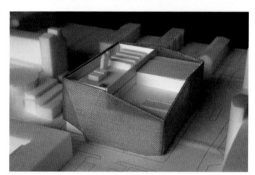

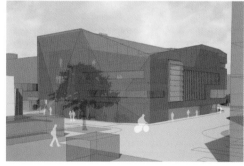

Initial façade proposals based on a copper finish

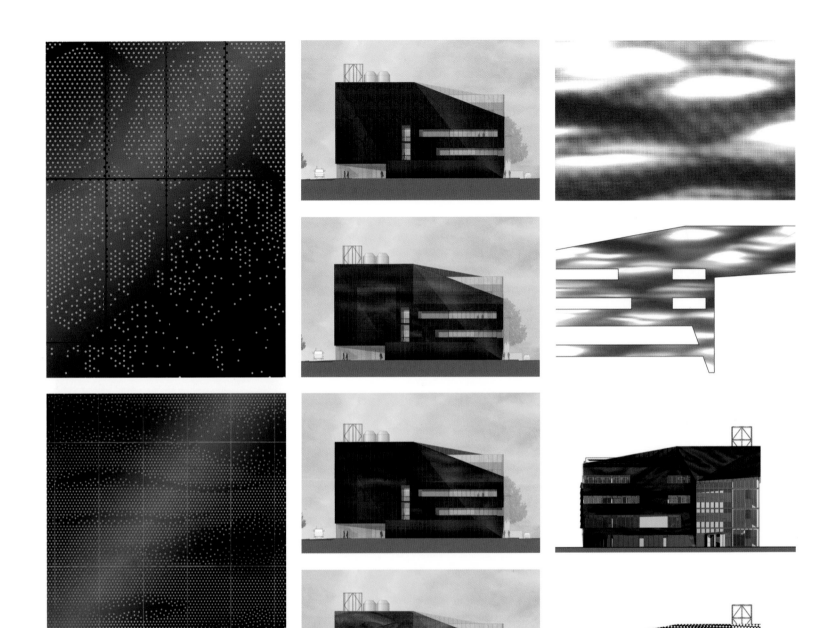

Developed façade studies

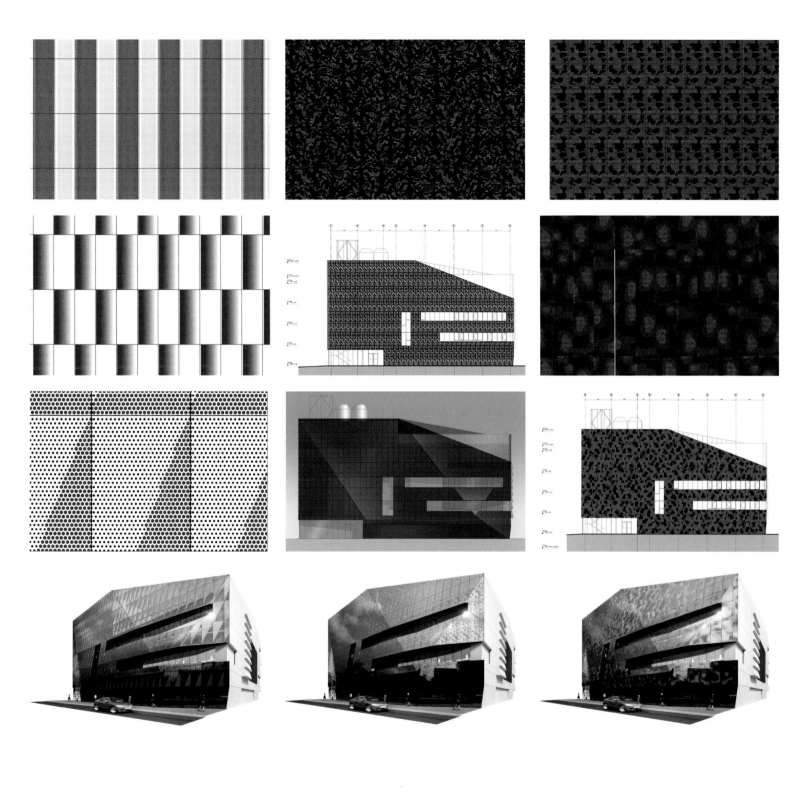

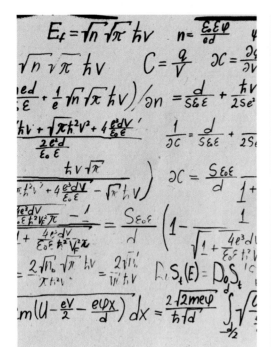
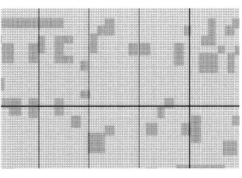
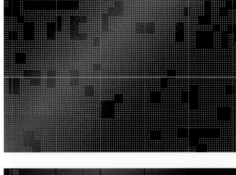

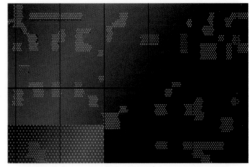
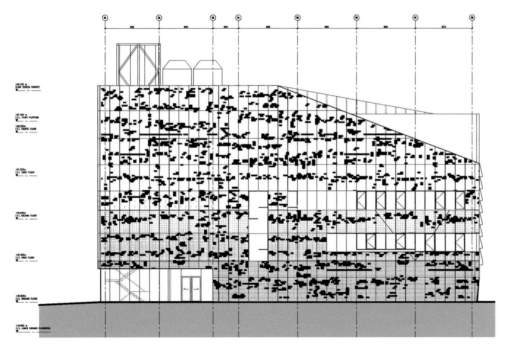
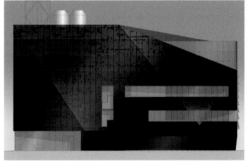

Options for 'the message'

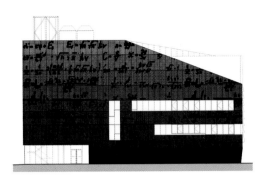 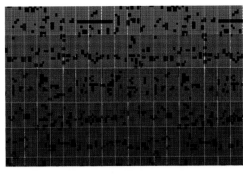 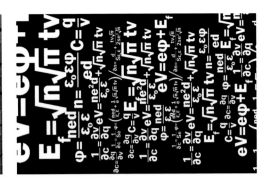

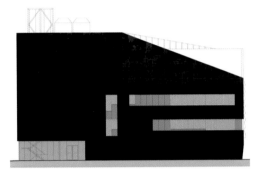  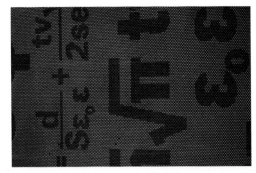

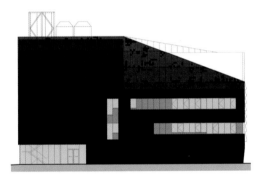

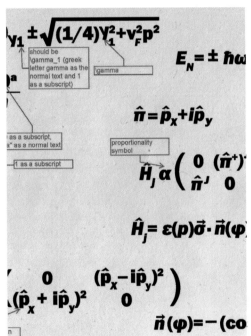

$$\gamma_1 \pm \sqrt{(1/4)\gamma_1^2 + v_F^2 p^2}$$

should be \gamma_1 (greek letter gamma as the normal text and 1 as a subscript)

\gamma

$$E_N = \pm\ \hbar\omega$$

a as a subscript, a" as a normal text

$$\hat{\pi} = \hat{p}_x + i\hat{p}_y$$

proportionality symbol

1 as a subscript

$$\hat{H}_J \propto \begin{pmatrix} 0 & (\hat{\pi}^+)^ \\ \hat{\pi}^J & 0 \end{pmatrix}$$

$$\hat{H}_J = \varepsilon(p)\vec{\sigma}\cdot\vec{n}(\varphi)$$

$$\begin{pmatrix} 0 & (\hat{p}_x - i\hat{p}_y)^2 \\ (\hat{p}_x + i\hat{p}_y)^2 & 0 \end{pmatrix}$$

$$\vec{n}(\varphi) = -(\text{co}$$

n

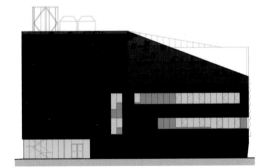 

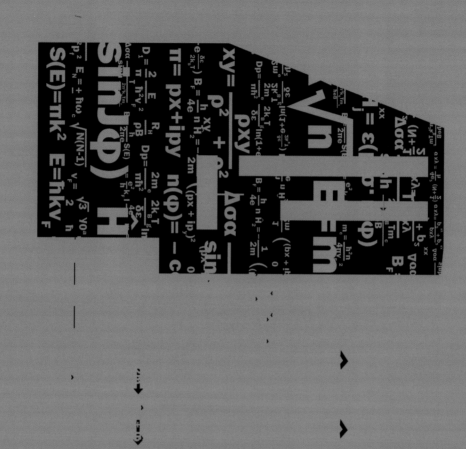

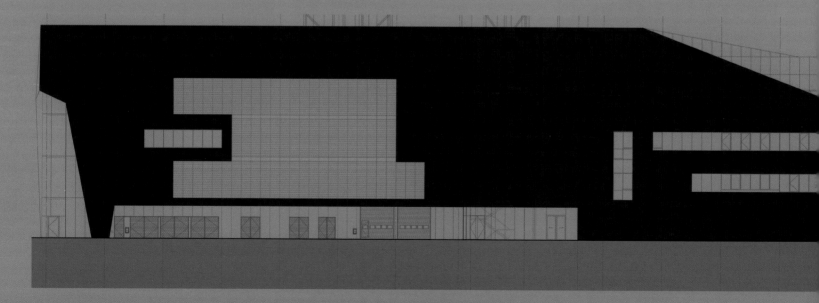

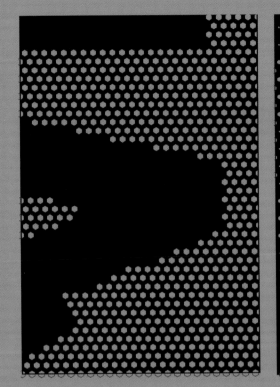

20% perforated

15% perforated

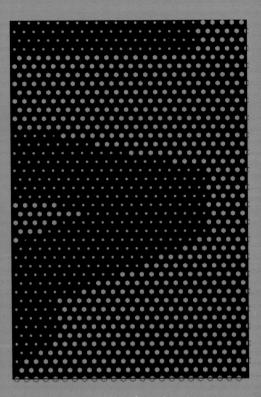

18% perforated

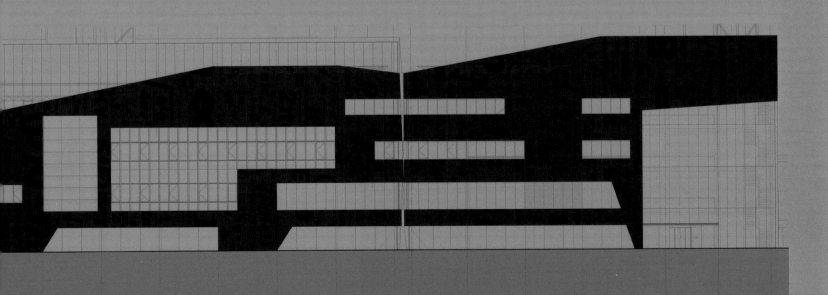

Professor Novoselov in
discussion with Tony Ling

Façade study model showing south elevation

Computer generated image of north elevation

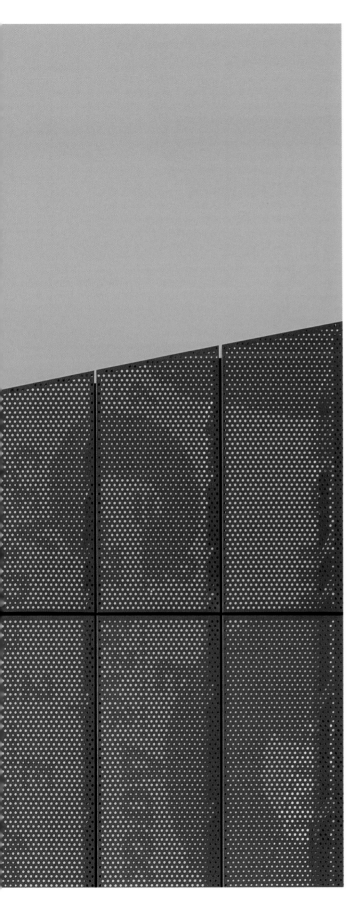

The right formula

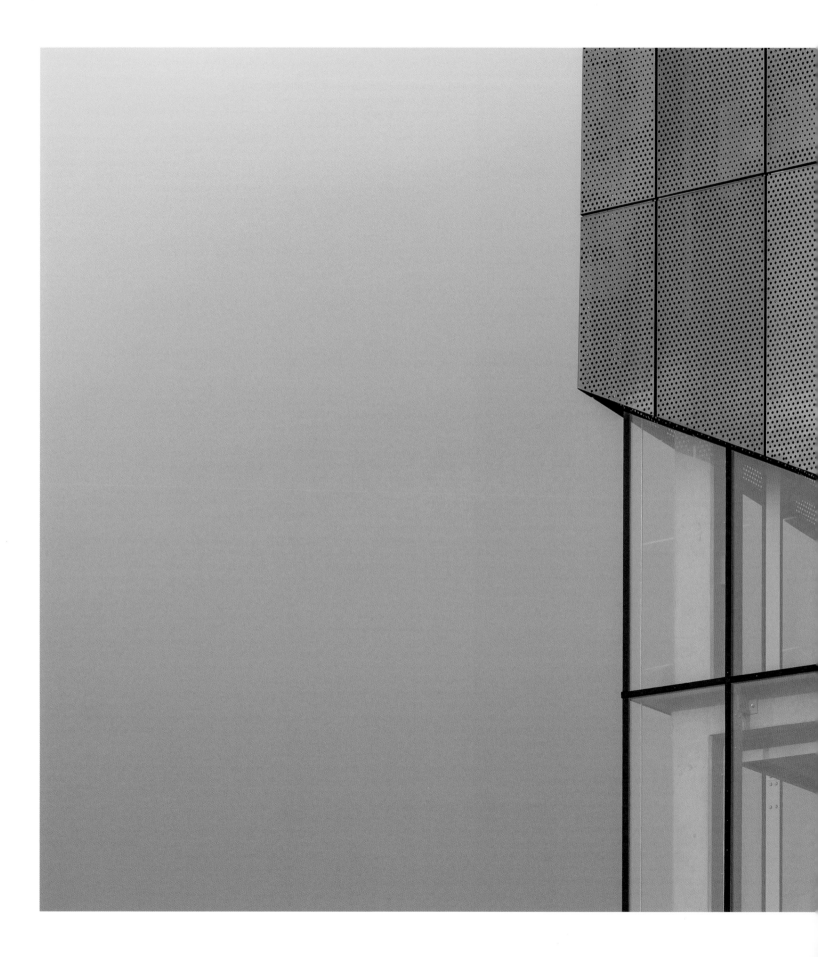

# The Engels' Sink

What connects the founders of
communism to graphene?

Remains of the terrace houses and the Albert Club uncovered during archeological survey

A sandstone sink uncovered by Professor Kostya Novoselov and his students in the remains of one of the terrace houses during the archeological survey

Engels' sink lives again in the seminar room

What connects the founders of communism to Graphene – a discovery that stands to become a worldwide commercial success? The answer is a small sink installed in the National Graphene Institute with a more interesting lineage than any other in the country, perhaps in the world.

The National Graphene Institute was constructed on the Booth Street East site where once stood the Albert Club, a gentleman's club which was established principally for the middle-class German community and businessmen involved in Manchester's cotton trade during the nineteenth century. One of that club's members was the then 22-year-old Friedrich Engels, who joined in 1842 and was in the city at that point to manage the factory of his father's textile firm, the Ermen & Engels Victoria Mill in Weaste. His father had sent the young firebrand to try to 'cure' him of his radical political views, but in the end it did the reverse - Engels was also keen to study in the most important industrial city in the world. He busied himself with an extensive study of the social conditions around him. Appalled by the poverty, child labour and slum conditions he saw around him in the city and elsewhere, Engels went on to write The Condition of the Working Class in England, based on his personal observations and research in Manchester, in 1845. And three years later he co-authored The Communist Manifesto with his more famous friend and colleague Karl Marx. Later the Albert Club would be converted into a Turkish public baths, and later still as a hospital for women and children. But over 50 years after its demolition in the 1960s, excavations made in 2013 prior to the construction of the NGI uncovered remnants of the Albert Club including steps and tiles along with a row of five cellars belonging to a row of 1830s terraced housing and cobbled streets in the area formerly known as Lawson Street. And, of course, that sink, which has been recovered and incorporated into the building.

Professor Novoselov told the local Manchester Evening News that he was immensely proud that the pioneering centre would be built on a site with a strong link to the Industrial Revolution as well as the emergence of a new social consciousness. 'We have been very careful to record these remnants of the Industrial Revolution and we will look to keep some artefacts for use in the new building or elsewhere', Novoselov told the paper. 'It is genuinely exciting.'

# From Seathwaite

A Wall Drawing by Mary Griffiths
permanently installed at
the National Graphene Institute

By Mary Griffiths

Within the hillside of Seathwaite Common in Borrowdale, Cumbria, lie the disused workings of many 'wad' or graphite mines. This was the first place in the world where graphite was found and from it developed a massive industry with men picking their way through the horizontal levels and vertical pipes of the mineral, people processing it on the valley floor, working it into pencils in nearby Keswick or sending it to be used in the casting of cannonballs and machinery. The gleam of graphite can still be seen on the walls of these mines, long worked out and abandoned for new finds in the Americas, India and China.

Specially commissioned by the National Graphene Institute, *From Seathwaite* is a wall drawing that is about the discovery of graphite in Borrowdale and also the isolation of graphene in a laboratory at The University of Manchester. This work of art is a permanent part of the NGI and was drawn directly on to the plaster on the wall of the building's atrium. Graphite was layered on by hand and then burnished to a high sheen. Into its dense blackness lines were cut by hand, revealing the white plaster beneath and delineating a 13m high abstract drawing. The topmost panel contains a zig-zag line and recalls the steep path that the miners had to climb up to the entrance of the mine. This white path edges down the wall and into the second panel, transforming into the hexagonal structure of a single atom of graphite/graphene. The third panel takes this single atom and grows it into a tessellation of graphene atoms, suggesting the revolutionary potential of this new material.

The drawing's highly polished black surface transforms the reflections of the internal architecture and the street outside. A steel beam becomes a hazy white line, a passing car's colour is caught fleetingly. Gazing at this vast drawing the viewer catches a glimpse of herself, a small speck of carbon mirrored within ancient geological strata and brand new science. In such a place, all things are possible.

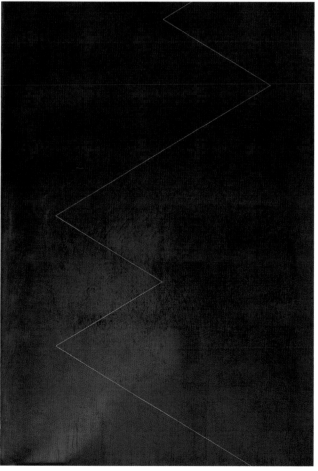

**From Seathwaite** 2015

**Artist**
Mary Griffiths

**Assisted by**
Nina Chua, Nicola Ellis,
Mark Kennard, Naomi Lethbridge

**Project Manager**
Sophia Crilly

**Photography**
Michael Pollard

**Commissioned by**
the National Graphene Institute,
The University of Manchester with
funding from Arts Council England

# How the Building Works

By Tony Ling

The spatial organisation of the National Graphene Institute is a direct response to its functionality, an arrangement that addresses technical and environmental requirements for the cleanrooms, laboratories, offices and ancillary spaces. Form following function. The building consists of two cleanrooms, 19 labs of different disciplines, including optical, laser, chemistry, electro-magnetic shielded room, prototyping room, 2 large open plan labs, as well as cellular, and shared academic offices, breakout areas, meeting rooms and a large multi-purpose seminar room.

One of the early and key design moves was to locate the large cleanroom on the lower ground floor, to achieve the best vibration performance. This set the scene for the development of all the floor plans, starting with the unusual arrangement that the ground floor became for the most part, a pressurised plenum – a walk-on ceiling plant room that serves the cleanroom below it. To obviate a completely blank street level façade, the edges of this 3m high enclosed ceiling space are angled back along the pavement to allow views down into the cleanroom, bringing daylight and views into the cleanroom via glazed walls that separate it from the surrounding viewing corridor. Other functions located on the ground floor include the two entrances, at opposite ends of the building, loading bay, goods, chemical and gas stores, and electrical substation and switch rooms.

Part of the main entrance forms a 2m wide slot that extends up the full height of the building, visually connecting the different floors behind the glazed front façade, particularly the breakout seating areas off the lift lobby on each floor.

Located on the first floor is the fully glazed 400m$^2$ second cleanroom which is connected to the main cleanroom on the lower ground floor via an internal clean lift, the only installation of its kind in Europe. The rest of the floor comprises a mix of flexible, modular labs of generally 6.6m x 6.6m, a 600m$^2$ open plan lab, cellular offices for 1 to 3 persons and larger offices accommodating 15 to 18 graduate students or post docs. The centrally located large open plan lab houses shared tools and equipment such as

measuring instruments and cryostats and provides opportunities for encounters between researchers as they use the common facilities. All the more so since most of the offices open onto and are accessed through this lab.

The majority of the labs face the outside with generous windows providing a good level of daylight and views. The exceptions are those requiring occlusion, typically laser and optical labs which are gathered in an internal block, adjacent to the open plan lab. All the offices are located along external walls and are naturally ventilated with openable windows.

The second floor is essentially a replica of the first, the arrangement allowing great flexibility of occupation by differently sized research groups and changing research directions and team composition over time. This is particularly important for the largely unpredictable trends in graphene research and the invited industry partners who are sharing the facility with the academics.

Forming the heart of the working environment and connecting the two central floors is a double height breakout space overlooked by labs and offices and linked by a feature spiral stair. Care was taken with the acoustic treatment and the space is lit by a full height sawtooth window. The window extends into a continuous roof light over the top of the space. It is also entirely naturally ventilated by a stack effect using low level opening windows and high level louvres along the edges of the roof light.

The top floor of the building steps back to form an L-shape plan, creating a south facing roof terrace which encompasses a bio-diverse roof garden in the centre. Opening onto the roof terrace on one side are offices and on the other a large multi-purpose seminar room/café/ common room. This room can be subdivided into two or three smaller spaces for a variety of uses and also serves as a public lecture and functions venue. The front part of the third floor also houses the building's suite of chemistry labs and furnace room.

## Ventilation

1 Air intake to plant

2 CUB

3 Plant

4 Cellular office

5 Air conditioned labs

6 Plenum

7 Air conditioned clean rooms

8 Fan filter unit within air plenum

9 Raised floor provides air return
to vertical chases

10 Low solar gain - morning sun

11 Motorised louvres connected
to building management system
with potential heat recovery system

12 Naturally ventilated breakout space

13 Void enables warm air to rise up
through 'stack' effect ventilation

## Sustainability

As agreed with Manchester City Council, the scheme
has been designed to achieve a BREEAM rating of 'Very
Good'. In addition, the university set a target of 65% -
10% higher than the minimum threshold for 'Very Good'.
The relatively high operational energy consumption over
the lifetime of the building is the principal consideration
for this building type. The design responds by employing
an efficient building form and organisation, a highly
insulated building envelope, highly efficient mechanical and
electrical systems and on-site renewable energy sources.

To meet strict environmental conditions required for the
research, the clean rooms and laboratories need to be
air conditioned with high air change rates and filtration.
The plant areas are housed within the multi-level Central
Utility Building (CUB) on the west side of the building.
This stacked arrangement of plant reduces the impact
of plant vibration on the research spaces, and is also
an energy efficient arrangement which reduces duct
and cable runs between equipment: the clean rooms
and laboratories are located adjacent to the CUB on
each level, with the offices, the most lightly serviced
areas of the building, furthest away from the CUB.

The offices are naturally ventilated with openable windows
and no backup mechanical ventilation systems. Radiators in
the offices give occupiers control of their own environment.
Exposed concrete soffits throughout provide thermal mass
and reduce diurnal temperature variations.

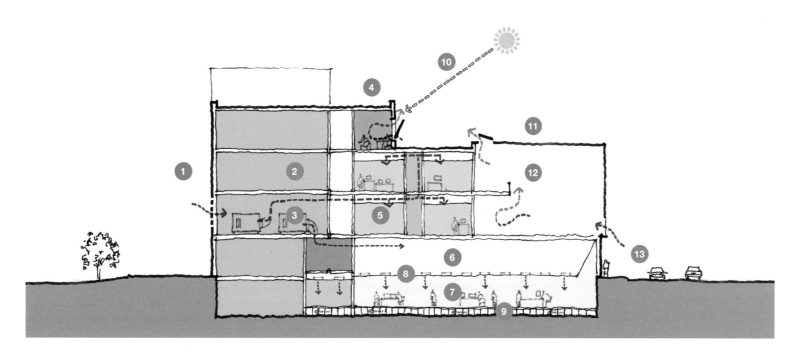

The breakout space makes use of stack effect to naturally ventilate, with low-level automatically opening windows to draw fresh air in, and high level roof light vents for releasing warmer air.

Good daylight and views are provided to all offices, with daylight or borrowed light to laboratories where appropriate. Low energy lighting has been used throughout, with motion sensors.

Target U-Values at design stage have been met through a highly insulated and airtight building envelope - values of $0.15W/m^2K$, $0.17W/m^2K$, $0.06W/m^2K$ and $1.44W/m^2K$ through the roof, walls, floor and windows respectively have been achieved by the construction.

20% of the electrical load is provided by on-site renewable energy sources, including photovoltaic panels located on the roof and a 900 kW steam fired Li-Br absorption chiller.

In addition, the design caters for future integration into a campus District Heating System which is under development.

To keep water consumption low, a rainwater harvesting tank located in the CUB captures and re-uses rainwater collected from the roof. Low water consumption sanitary appliances are also used throughout the building and an attenuation tank delays the release of rainwater to the mains drainage system. A green roof is provided on the third floor terrace which has matured into a thriving bio-diverse mini-ecosystem since being installed.

To encourage staff and visitors to walk, jog or cycle to the facility, an extension to the existing lockable cycle store provides 20 secure, covered cycle parking spaces. Showers and lockers are also provided for walkers, joggers and cyclists.

Further information on the services design is available within the CIBSE article
http://www.cibsejournal.com/case-studies/the-home-of-graphene/

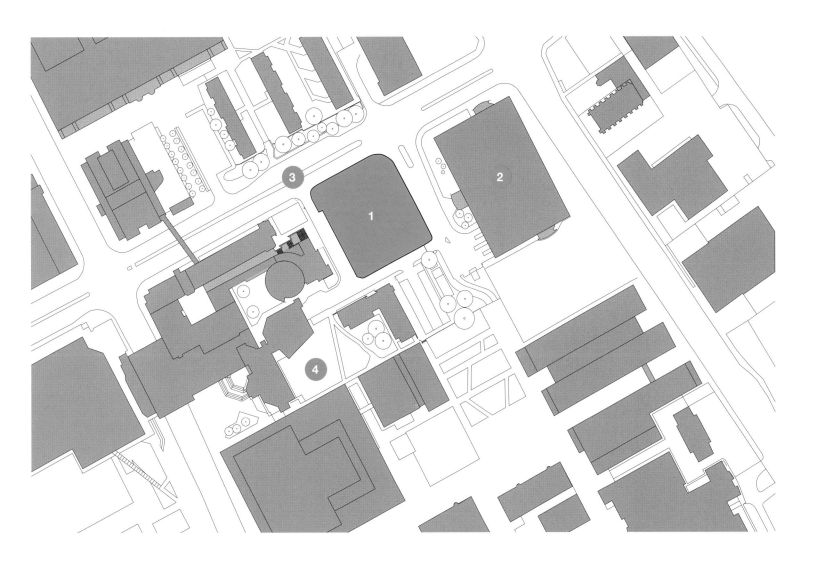

**Location Plan**

1 National Graphene Institute

2 Multi-storey car park

3 Booth Street East

4 University buildings

BB ■

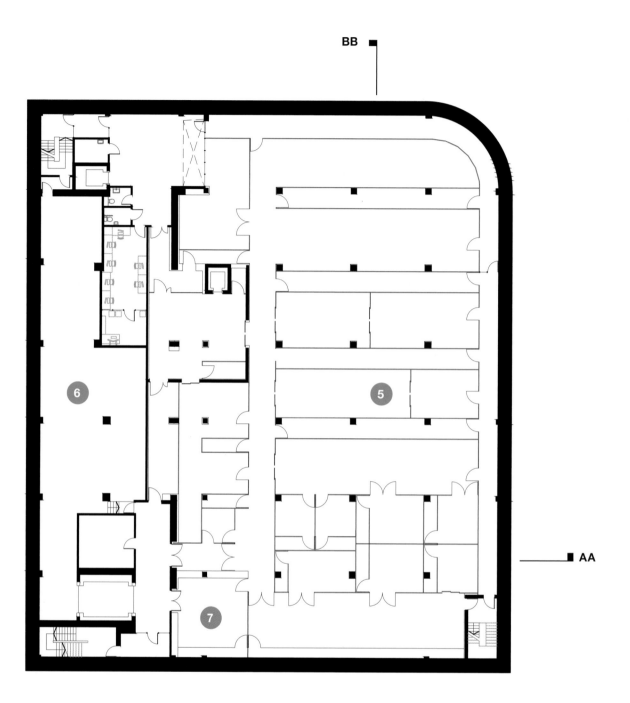

■ AA

**Basement**

5 Cleanrooms

6 Plant

7 Optical lab

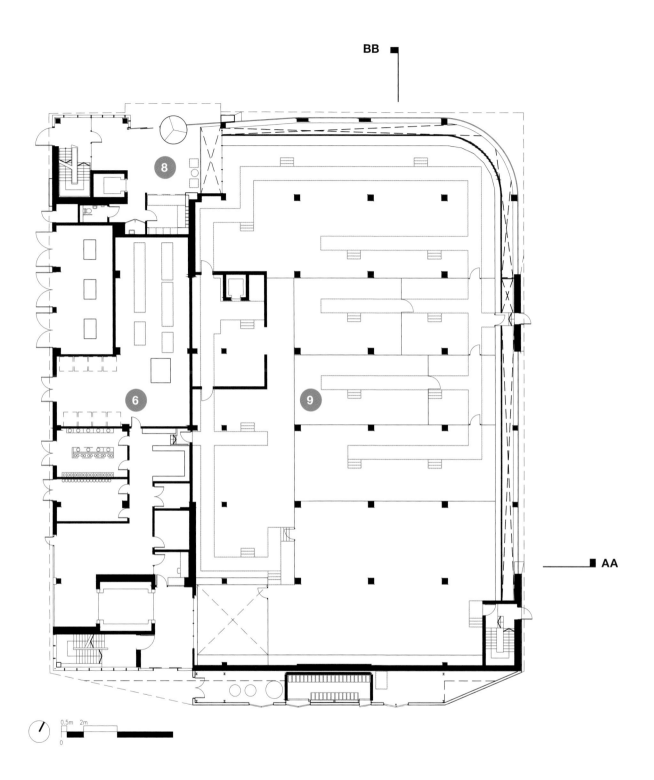

**Ground Floor**

6 Plant

8 Main entrance

9 Plenum

**First Floor**

| | | |
|---|---|---|
| **5** Cleanrooms | **10** Research lab | **15** Breakout |
| **6** Plant | **11** Open-plan lab | |
| **7** Optical lab | **12** Offices | |

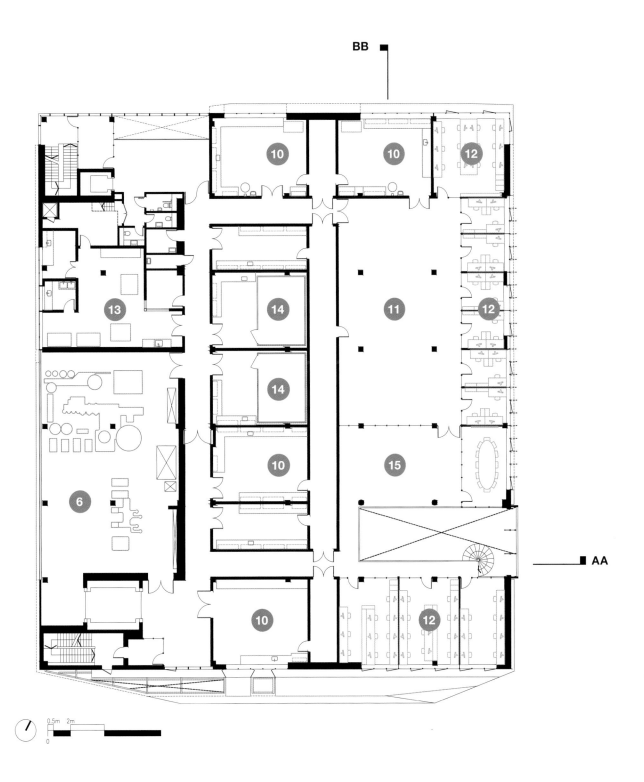

**Second Floor**

| | | |
|---|---|---|
| 6 Plant | 12 Offices | 15 Breakout |
| 10 Research lab | 13 Prototyping room | |
| 11 Open-plan lab | 14 Shielded room | |

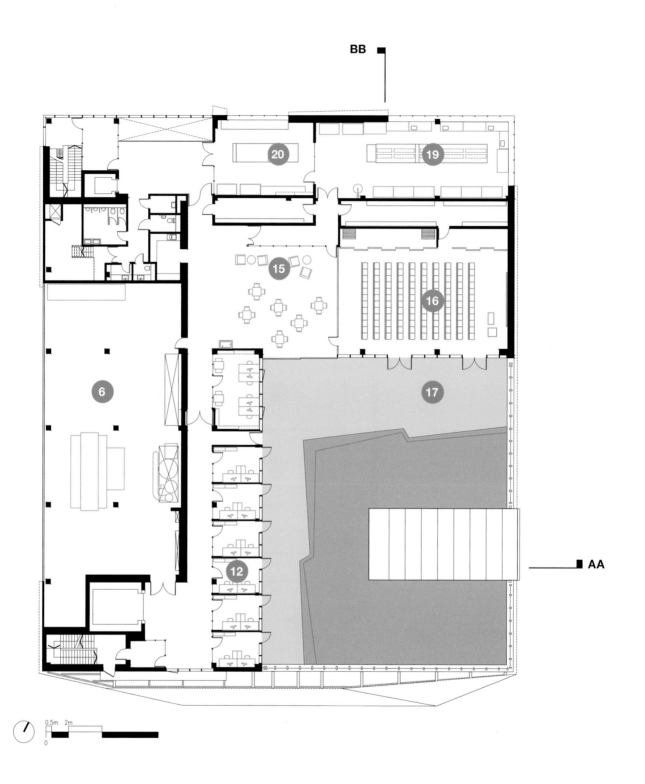

**BB** ■

■ **AA**

0.5m  2m

0

**Third Floor**

6 Plant

12 Offices

15 Breakout

16 Seminar room

17 Roof terrace

19 Chemistry lab

20 Furnace room

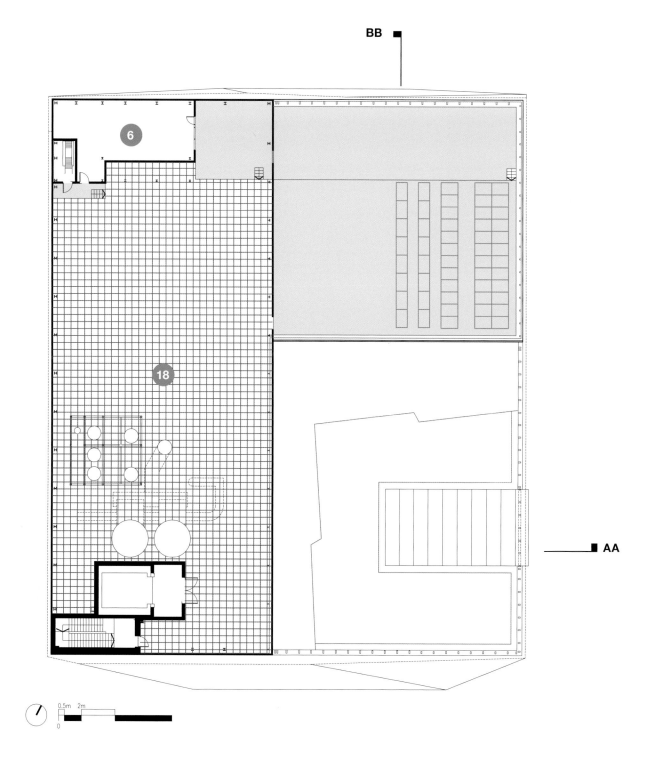

BB ■

■ AA

0.5m 2m
0

**Fouth Floor / Roof**

6 Plant

18 Rooftop plant zone

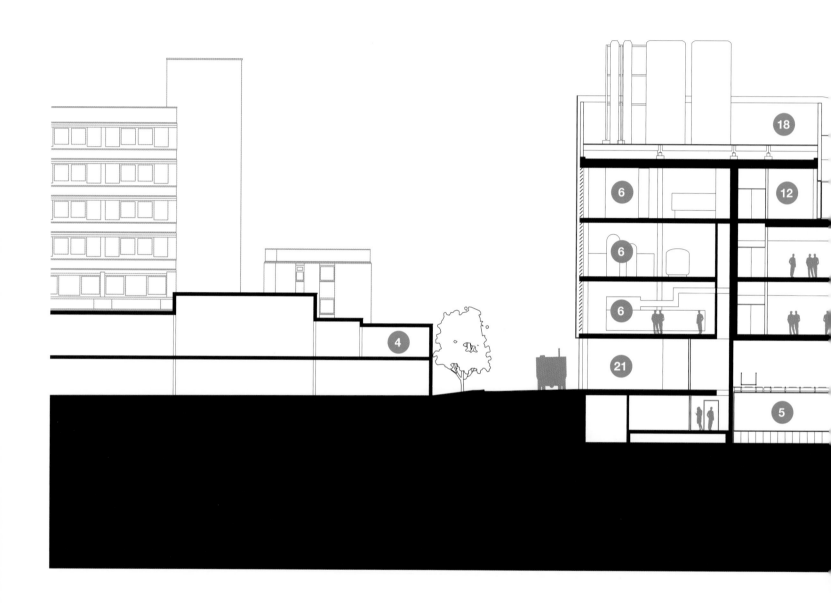

**Section AA**

2 Multi-storey car park

4 University buildings

5 Cleanrooms

6 Plant

9 Plenum

15 Breakout

17 Roof terrace

18 Rooftop plant zone

21 Loading bay

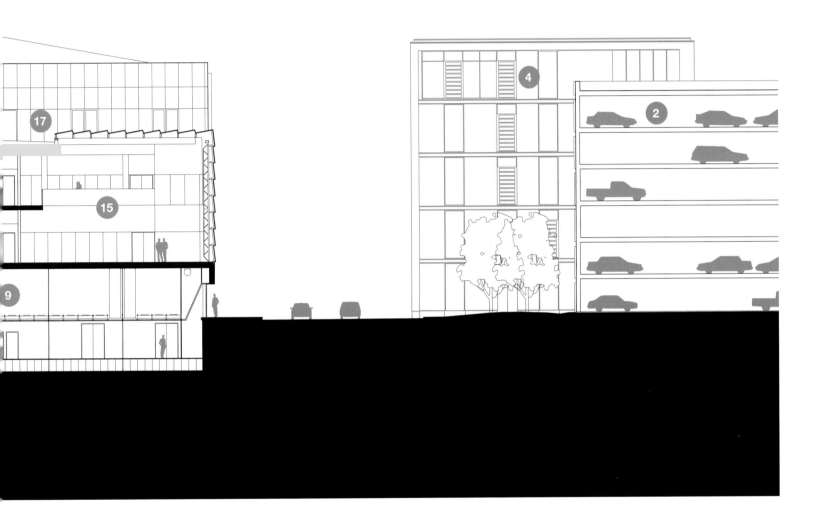

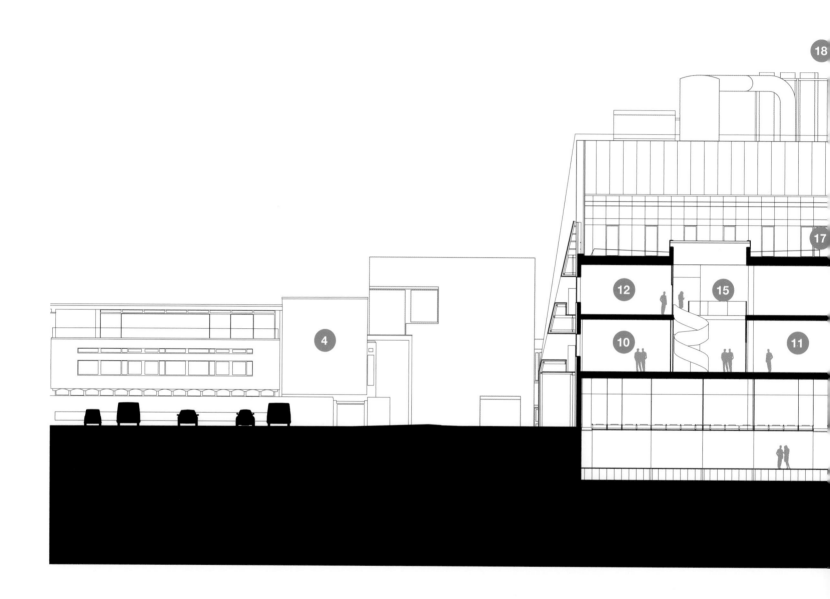

**Section BB**

3 Booth Street East

4 University buildings

5 Cleanrooms

9 Plenum

10 Research lab

11 Open-plan lab

12 Offices

15 Breakout

16 Seminar room

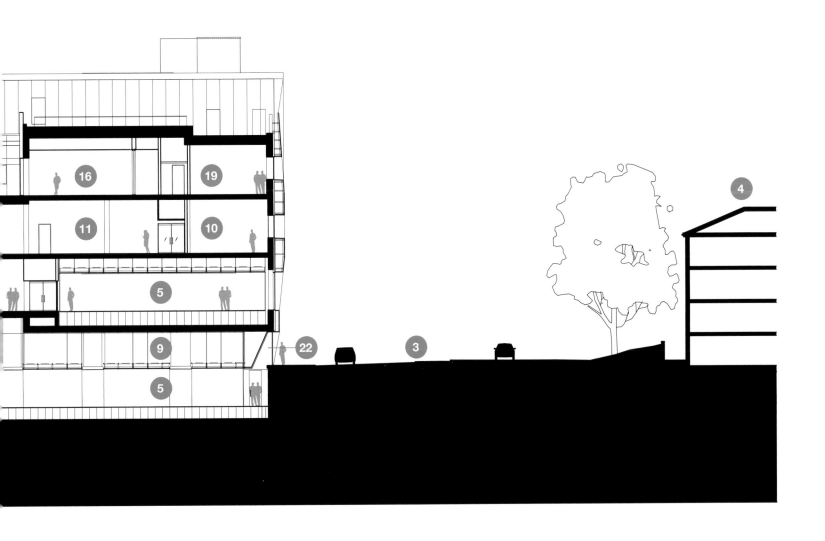

17 Roof terrace

18 Rooftop plant zone

19 Chemistry lab

22 Viewing corridors

## The Future

---

'I'm looking at it from how
exciting is it, research-wise.'

**Graphene contact lens**
Graphene could be used to develop 'smart' contact lenses and night vision

**Graphene coating**
This house brick has been half coated with graphene paint which is impermeable to water

**Graphene electronics** (left)
Faster transistors and semiconductors, even bendable phones are all possible with graphene

**Graphene membranes** (right)
Graphene membranes can be used for desalination, filtering out pollutants from drinking water

Like aluminium, which only really came of age when it was used in aeroplane design, graphene remains a material that hasn't yet found its real niche. There are ideas to capitalise on its many properties and use it in bicycles, in mobiles, biomedical, anti-tamper solutions for wine bottles, even to mop up nuclear waste. A Masters student from Manchester even tested the graphene tennis racquet made by Head and used by world number one Novak Djokovic. Yes, it has graphene in it, and the makers claim it is to redistribute weight more efficiently into the head and grip rather than the shaft, where graphene lends its strength.

Novoselov himself is consulted as 'an educator' by many of the world's leading firms. 'We work with lots of commercial companies. We passed the hype stage a long time ago.' But the problem with science, says Novoselov, is you are trying to do something completely unknown to you. You need a work plan and a goal. 'And what you hope is you will never reach it because you will be side-tracked by another discovery.' The road map changes continuously, adds Novoselov, but then that is the nature of road maps.

The original goal was to make a transistor, before graphene came along. But perhaps, like aluminium, we won't really know for perhaps decades what its true use or uses will be. 'What people are trying to do now is to use it as a replacement material for other materials in existing applications. But ideally you would design a completely new application which would use all those properties and would require exactly the same thinking out of the box as the process which initially created this material. It hasn't exactly happened yet, but is happening now in completely new areas'.

One way is in the research into smart RFIDs (Radio-Frequency Identification often used to track tags attached to objects) combined with sensor applications; antennae could be used to monitor certain parameters. This could range from how much you might be sweating, to perhaps a monitor that can tell you when your milk is about to turn by sending a message to the fridge that its PH has changed. RFIDs can be printed onto pretty much anything – the next step that Novoselov is working on is applying for a patent to print onto clothes and then print together with sensors. Work is also underway into investigating graphene's potential for use in filtration and separation, optical devices, and a whole host of other uses. The potential for graphene applications is only limited by time and imagination, in fact. 'I'm the wrong person to ask, because academics are the last people you want to run your business', Novoselov laughs. 'I'm looking at it from how exciting is it, research-wise.' Manufacturing is a different story. But in the end, one of the primary purposes of the National Graphene Institute – part of its DNA – is to get both academia and business to speak to each other more, for their mutual benefit.

And ultimately, for ours.

## Selected Publications

---

'Graphene Architecture' published
in Physics World

'Material World' published
in Architecture Today

# Graphene Architecture

by Kostya Novoselov and Tony Ling

This text first appeared in Physics World magazine's Focus on Nanotechnology, published in June 2013

Think about a typical physics research laboratory and an image comes to mind of a place that is full of equipment – probably quite messy – with several experiments going on at the same time and with the flexibility to accommodate even more. But an industrial lab, designed for one particular technological process, will be much tidier, more organized, more efficiently run and less prone to being altered. As for the architects who develop such buildings, they come with slick designs, keen to make sure the labs look as good on the outside as on the inside – and desperate to understand what their clients really want and provide the best possible solution to their needs.

So what happens when these three groups – scientists, engineers and architects – come together to design a new building for academics to work with business people and push exciting discoveries from fundamental science into real-world products? The result is a melting pot of ideas, views and thoughts, coupled with plenty of delicate compromises, and lots of interesting and novel architectural solutions. At least that has been the experience for both of us in designing the UK's new National Graphene Institute (NGI) at the University of Manchester.

The NGI was first announced by the UK government in 2011 as part of its plan to build a nationwide 'graphene hub' with the NGI at its centre. Intended to facilitate the transition of graphene technology from laboratory to production, the NGI will host researchers from different disciplines, as well as engineers from external companies, to bring about intensive technology transfer. Construction of the five-storey, £61m building – funded by the Engineering and Physical Sciences Research Council and the European Union – is set to begin this year and to open in early 2015. In planning the building, the architects held intensive briefing sessions with key researchers who will work in the NGI, as well as with members of the university's estates team, building managers, maintenance officers and security staff. This has been a long, iterative process that started on day one of the design project and will continue while the building is built – and even beyond. Our goal throughout has been to strike the right balance between having a research space that is flexible enough to deal with future unknown requirements, yet is solid and stable enough to support current tools and experimental equipment.

With so many challenging requirements and interested parties, it is natural that many demands proved to be mutually contradictory – requiring elegant, delicate solutions and a fair degree of compromise. In particular, the researchers' requests for spacious labs, extended services and flexibility collided with demands from estates officers that the labs be easy to maintain and service. And both sides' wishes have in turn been stymied by ever-more burdensome health-and-safety restrictions. At the same time, all parties want to create a building that is as cheap as possible to build but that will be a stunning landmark and visually arresting for years to come.

### A flexible approach

Graphene is a fascinating material with a number of unique properties that is attracting the attention of thousands of physicists, chemists and materials scientists around the world. First isolated in 2004 by one of us (KN) working with Andre Geim, the material is not only the strongest ever discovered, but also the stiffest, and can sustain a current density a million times that of copper. Graphene is a disruptive technology that is expected to contribute to many existing applications and, hopefully, create many novel ones too.

But with graphene research developing so fast and diversifying into a plethora of new directions, any facility designed to support both research and applications has many conflicting demands. The major challenge in designing the NGI was that the building not only needs to support certain specific scientific and engineering projects, but also has to be flexible – capable of adapting quickly to support, say, new interdisciplinary collaborations, new equipment or new experiments. We also wanted the NGI to encourage researchers to innovate and deploy new experimental techniques with the minimum of time and effort (especially when fighting against today's increasingly stringent health-and-safety regulations).

To meet these long-term, wide-ranging aspirations, the NGI building will have two huge cleanrooms (one 1100m$^2$ and the other 400m$^2$) plus a total of 1500m$^2$ of laboratory space with many features that can easily be adapted if researchers want to move in new directions. The cleanrooms will have tiled, removable floors to allow equipment to be installed or repositioned with ease, along with interior walls that can be demounted and reconfigured

at will, and mechanical and electrical support that allows the level of cleanliness to be adjusted to suit changing research needs. But for maximum flexibility, the entire floor of the larger cleanroom (to be used by university researchers) has been designed to meet or exceed what are known as 'vibration curve-D criteria', which will permit the most vibration-sensitive and demanding research equipment to be located anywhere in the cleanroom.

We have done this by positioning the cleanrooms directly on the bedrock, which lies more than 4m below street level. The rest of the basement space – also on the bedrock – will be home to a vibration-sensitive optics and laser lab.

### A place for everyone

Research into graphene is such a multidisciplinary activity that in designing the NGI we have to make sure that its labs can support workers from many different specialisations. Scientists seeking new ways of making graphene, for example, will require large furnaces and chemistry facilities. Others processing graphene will need large cleanrooms of varying specifications, while those studying the electrical or optical properties of the material will want labs with specialised equipment. We have therefore had to think hard about how to combine these facilities so that people from different fields can collaborate, while at the same time minimising interference so that stray magnetic fields from the labs do not hamper electron-beam lithography in a cleanroom, for example.

The NGI therefore has modular labs – each with a floor space of about 50 m$^2$ and equipped with modular racking and shelving – that can be tailored to specific research needs. Each lab also has an adjoining 'grey space' to house pumps, compressors and any other noisy or dirty equipment, and to provide storage areas and the main distribution routes for services into the labs.

In addition, the NGI will have two other large open-plan labs with offices along one side, which the researchers can access via the lab space. We hope that this design will impart a sense of community to the research environment, while large windows – covering the full available wall width – will be provided (where possible) to bring natural daylight into the labs and let scientists look outside. Both aspects were considered to be of paramount importance to their work-space by the users.

A similar challenge arose in deciding where to locate the offices and labs, which need to be nearby to stimulate experimental activity and make workflow more efficient, but also flexible enough to accommodate people from different groups. The layout of the building was made more complex still by the fact that it will also be occupied by both academics and engineers from industrial companies. Although there will be no actual commercial activity in the NGI, the companies using the building will obviously want a certain level of privacy and labs that meet industrial standards. The current plan is to invite about half a dozen leading manufacturers to carry out collaborative research projects with university researchers. Immersing industrial partners into the day-to-day operation of the NGI will create an efficient two-way traffic of technologies.

### Doing business

All work and no play would make very dull scientists. The NGI will therefore contain relaxation areas consisting of a top-lit, double-height breakout space in the centre of the building (which could potentially be reconfigured for use as a lab if required) and a large multipurpose seminar and social area on the top floor. The breakout space, which connects the two main laboratory floors by a spiral staircase, is overlooked on three sides by labs and offices, and has the largest single window in the building. It is an area for researchers to meet away from their labs and we hope that the relaxed atmosphere will promote the serendipitous exchange of ideas that is the lifeblood of so many scientific breakthroughs.

The building's one publicly accessible area is a seminar suite on the top floor. It includes a subdivisible room that can be used for formal lectures, receptions or board meetings, and also contains a cafe and common room. The area opens out onto a south-facing roof terrace and garden as an additional amenity. Fixed to the outside of the building's inner skin, meanwhile, is a separate perforated stainless-steel 'veil' that wraps continuously around the structure to provide a unifying texture and coherent, fluid shape. Shadows from the perforations in the veil will cast interesting and continually changing shadows onto the inner façades of the NGI – creating an image of an abstract, complex and somewhat mysterious scientific research facility, without being overtly symbolic.

Other interesting features of the NGI that will make it easier for scientists to convert their ideas into potential commercial products include a 'prototyping workshop', which would streamline the production of prototype graphene-based devices, and special chemistry and furnace facilities for scaling up the production of graphene. We have also tried hard to make sure that researchers at the NGI can move swiftly into new fields while still satisfying health-and-safety regulations, such as open-air space for storing toxic or asphyxiating gases, which would let scientists introduce

new technological recipes without needing expensive oxygen and gas sensors. Using movable panels for the walls in some labs will also allow large equipment to be easily incorporated.

Designing the NGI has been a long, involved and challenging process, in which many interesting and efficient solutions have already been incorporated, and to which others will be dreamed up when the construction phase begins. But the long hours of discussions and brainstorming by architects and the building's future users – the researchers themselves – have ensured that the design accurately reflects the spirit of the NGI as a place for exciting science and innovation, where unconventional ideas can flow unimpeded and where multidisciplinary research and technology transfer are the norm. We hope that many researchers will be happy to call the NGI not just a workplace but their home.

# Material World

by Roger Hawkins

This text first appeared in the September 2015 issue
of Architecture Today

Last year, the centenary of stainless steel was celebrated in Sheffield. Its initial discovery has been credited to Harry Brearley who added chromium to molten iron to produce a metal that did not rust. However, the commercial application of this new material progressed at a relatively slow pace and it was not until the Art Deco period that the use of stainless steel in buildings became popular, most famously with the upper portion of the Chrysler building in 1929. Across the Pennines in Manchester there is a desire to benefit from a new super material with considerably more urgency. Manchester wants to be known as 'Graphene City' and it is investing heavily into research and production of the world's thinnest, strongest and most conductive material.

The £61m National Graphene Institute (NGI) provides a focus for academic research, seeking collaboration with specialists to investigate incredible opportunities made possible since physicists Sir Andre Geim and Sir Kostya Novoselov first isolated the one-atom-thick material from graphite at The University of Manchester in 2004. The next facility, set to open in 2017 will be the £60m Graphene Engineering Innovation Centre (GEIC) aiming to establish industry-led developments in graphene applications such as lightweight batteries you can wear, smartphones you can bend or paint that can generate power. One of the simplest ways to harness graphene's outstanding properties is to create composites. This could result in even more expensive bicycles or the world's lightest plane made from graphene fibre.

The NGI was designed by Jestico + Whiles, and on a recent tour with project associate Jennifer de Vere-Hopkins I was able to look at a flake of graphene through a scanning electron microscope. It is a big building for such a small amount of matter. At 7,825 square metres it comprises 1,500 square metres of cleanrooms (class 100 and 1000) which have an atmosphere more than a million times purer than outside air and the latest technology for nano-scale projects. Such facilities need to minimise any vibrations and this is most cost-effectively achieved by digging out a basement and anchoring the structure to a stable layer of shale four metres below the ground.

Consequently, almost the entire ground floor becomes a service area, with the entrance and reception relegated to a corner location, along with the stair. A perimeter viewing corridor allows a glimpse from the street into the basement, but offers little by way of active frontage onto Booth Street East or the entrance to the University of Manchester's main campus.

Up to 120 researchers occupy the building, many of them wearing blue body suits and travelling from the basement cleanroom to a second facility on the third floor via a special clean lift, which is the first of its kind to be installed in the UK. Elsewhere are laser, optical, metrology and chemical labs.

Within the five-storey building, two structurally independent frames minimise the transfer of vibrations that could interfere with the experimental work taking place. Noise, dust or light are also potential contagions which need to be controlled, making for a highly clinical environment. Even the 'chalk board' is black glass with a white marker pen to avoid dust and squeaking. Normally this requirement for unobjectionableness would result in a bland interior, yet the architects have managed to find small pockets of joy throughout the building. An informal seminar room opens out onto a rooftop terrace where The University of Manchester's Biodiversity group has planted neat signs to explain in detail how bee-sensitive flowers have been selected for the green roof. And a sandstone sink salvaged from the site by Sir Kostya and his students has been re-used in the staff room as a permanent reminder of the city's industrial past.

So-called 'grey space', located between the laboratories, allows technicians to control every aspect of the internal environment without entering the cleanrooms. The intricate detailing and precise layout of pipes and conduits is a work of art kept hidden from most visitors. More visible as an art installation is a full-height graphite panel by Mary Griffiths over several floors of the entrance lobby. An inscribed line shows a tessellation of graphene, representing the way in which the material's structure gives it great strength. The local Whitworth Art Gallery also commissioned Cornelia Parker to make a work of art from graphene. Microscopic samples were made from specks of graphite collected by Novoselov from drawings by William Blake, Turner, Constable and Picasso, as well as a pencil-written letter by Sir Ernest Rutherford (who split the atom in Manchester). The graphene fragments were then launched in a firework display at a spectacular opening earlier this year.

Back on earth, the building stands out against its institutional neighbours with a striking polished black-mirrored Rimex stainless steel cladding forming a rainscreen over an inner skin of structural glazing and silver Eurobond cladding panels. This outer 'veil' is folded to suggest an abstract representation of graphene, together with a visual manifestation of handwritten formulas relating to its properties. On the sunny day I visited, the pixelated graphics laser-cut into the stainless steel were clearly visible, a subtle nod to Harry Brearley who could not have imagined that his desire for 'rustless steel cutlery' could be transformed into such a large-scale cloak shielding the incredible academic research being undertaken inside the NGI.

# The NGI Team

## Construction and Design Team

**Client**
The University of Manchester
Project Manager: Stuart Lockwood

**Civil and Structural Engineer**
Ramboll
Director: Ben Rowe
Lead Engineer: Emily Duncombe

**M+E Engineer**
CH2M
Electrical Engineer: Ian MacAaskill
Mechanical Engineers:
Tom Schmolke, Stephen Wright

**Project Manager & QS**
Arcadis
Project Manager: Mel Manku
Cost Manager: Ian Aldous

**Fire Consultant**
Ramboll
Fire Engineer: Peter Muir

**Acoustics Consultant**
Ramboll Acoustic
Engineer: Paul Driscoll

**Access Consultant**
David Bonnett Associates
Access Consultant:
Stuart Schlindwein-Robinson

**CDM Co-ordinator**
Keelagher Okey Klein
CDM Coordinator: Paul Jones

**Approved Inspector**
HCD
Project Manager: Steve Highwood

**Main Contractor**
BAM North West
Project Director: Tony Grindrod

**Architect**
Jestico + Whiles
CH2M

Tony Ling
Julian Dickens
Jennifer de Vere-Hopkins
Allan Thomson
Archna Patel
Aditi Saxena
Alicja Kubis
Bob Hedivan
Bruno Chialastri
Emily Baker
Graham MacKenzie
Heinz Richardson
Jakub Loucka
Javier Estevez
Kum-Min Kim
Laura Lupo
Lorraine Griffith
Louise Proudman
Lukas Kasprowicz
Michael Evans
Michael Kloihofer
Peter McRoberts
Ross Beaton
Ruth McMahon
Simon Lowe
Tom Wildbore

## Design awards received at time of printing

**2016 RIBA Awards**
National Award Winner

**2016 RIBA Awards**
North West Regional Award Winner

**2015 Civic Trust Awards**
Commendation Winner

**2015 British Construction Industry Awards**
Major Building Project of the Year Award Winner

**2015 Schüco Excellence Awards for Design & Innovation**
Award Winner

**2015 North West Regional Construction Awards**
BIM Project of the Year Award Winner

# The Right Formula

## Photo and Illustration Credits

Alexander Liew
pages 5, 10, 35
Aurélien Thomas
pages 19, 20, 29
Chris Foster
page 14
Colin Boulter
page 14
Colin McPherson
(Neilson Reeves Photography)
page 16
Conrad Gesner
page 30
Daniel Shearing
pages 49, 50, 54, 57, 58, 78, 80, 111, 114, 121, 126
Hufton + Crow
pages 36, 43, 44, 45, 46, 52, 56, 60, 61, 64, 94, 96, 98, 117, 118, 122, 124
Jannik C. Meyer
page 31
Jestico + Whiles
All architectural drawings
Jill Jennings
page 32
Michael Pollard
pages 87, 88, 89, 90, 91
Peter Cook
page 40
The University of Manchester
pages 14, 22, 23, 32, 33, 112

Every effort has been made to trace the copyright holders, but if any have been inadvertently overlooked the necessary arrangements will be made at the earliest opportunity.

## Book Design and Editing

Alex Gordon
Aurélien Thomas
Jenny Gray
Kostya S. Novoselov
Tony Ling

Jestico + Whiles is grateful for the invaluable contributions and assistance from the following individuals, amongst others, which have made this book possible:

Professor Novoselov for his encouragement, advice and support as well as text and image contribution, David Taylor for producing the main text, Aurélien Thomas for the concept and graphic design of the book, and Mary Griffith for providing words and images for her work From Seathwaite.